Volume B

Focus on Grammar

An **Advanced** Course for Reference and Practice

Jay Maurer

Sharon Hilles, grammar consultant

Longman

Focus on Grammar: An Advanced Course for Reference and Practice, Volume B

Editorial Director: Joanne Dresner
Senior Development Editor: Joan Saslow
Assistant Editor: Jessica Miller
Production Editorial: Lisa Hutchins
Text Design: Six West Design
Cover Design: A Good Thing, Inc.
Book Production: Circa 86, Inc.
Text Art: Alex Bloch, Circa 86, Meryl Treatner

ISBN 0-201-82585-6

7 8 9 10-CRK-99

For Thain and Zeya

Contents

Focus on Grammar: An Advanced Course for Reference and Practice

Volume B

Appendices

About the Author

Jay Maurer has taught EFL in colleges, universities, and binational centers in the Somali Republic, Spain, Portugal, and Mexico. He has taught ESL in Washington State and at Columbia University's American Language Program. In addition, he was professor of college composition and literature for seventeen years at Santa Fe Community College and Northern New Mexico Community College. He is the coauthor of the popular and widely used series *Structure Practice in Context.* Currently he writes and teaches in Seattle.

Focus on Grammar: An Advanced Course for Reference and Practice has grown out of the author's experiences as a practicing teacher of both ESL and college writing.

Introduction

Focus on Grammar: An Advanced Course for Reference and Practice is the advanced text in the innovative *Focus on Grammar* series. Written by practicing ESL professionals, the series focuses on English grammar through lively listening, speaking, reading, and writing activities. Each of the four Student's Books is accompanied by a Workbook, Cassettes, and a Teacher's Manual. Software is also available. Each Student's Book stands alone as a complete text in itself or can be used as part of the *Focus on Grammar* series.

Both Controlled and Communicative Practice

Research in applied linguistics suggests that students expect and need to learn the formal rules of a language. However, students need to practice new structures in a variety of contexts to help them internalize and master these structures. To this end, *Focus on Grammar* provides an abundance of both controlled and communicative exercises so that students can bridge the gap between knowing grammatical structures and using them. The many communicative activities in each unit enable students to personalize what they have learned in order to talk to each other with ease about hundreds of everyday issues.

A Unique Four-Step Approach

The series follows a unique four-step approach. The first step is **contextualization.** New structures are shown in the natural context of passages, articles, and dialogues. This is followed by **presentation** of structures in clear and accessible grammar charts and explanations. The third step is **focused practice** of both form and meaning in numerous and varied controlled exercises. In the fourth step, students engage in **communication practice,** using the new structures freely and creatively in motivating, open-ended activities.

A Complete Classroom Text and Reference Guide

A major goal in the development of *Focus on Grammar* has been to provide a Student's Book that serves not only as a vehicle for classroom instruction but also as a resource for self-study. The combination of grammar charts, grammar notes, and extensive appendices provides a complete and invaluable reference guide for the student at the advanced level. Exercises in the Focused Practice sections of each unit are ideal for individual study, and students can check their work by using the complete Answer Key at the back of the book.

Thorough Recycling

Underpinning the scope and sequence of the series as a whole is the belief that students need to use target structures many times in many contexts at increasing levels of difficulty. For this reason, new grammar is constantly recycled so that students will feel thoroughly comfortable with it.

Comprehensive Testing Program

SelfTests at the end of each of the eight parts of the Student's Book allow for continual assessment of progress. In addition, diagnostic and final tests in the Teacher's Manual provide a ready-made, ongoing evaluation component for each student.

PART AND UNIT FORMAT

Focus on Grammar: An Advanced Course for Reference and Practice is divided into eight parts comprising twenty-one units. Each part contains grammatically related units, with each unit focusing on a specific grammatical structure or related groups of structures.

In this advanced-level text, some structures are grouped together because of their related application to writing. The infinitive of purpose, for example, is taught together with participial phrases because both kinds of structures function adverbially. But, more importantly, they have similar applications to the acquisition of two important concepts: sentence combining and avoiding dangling modifiers.

Each unit has one or more major themes relating the exercises to one another and providing a context that serves as a vehicle for the structure. All units have the same clear, easy-to-follow format:

Introduction

The Introduction presents the grammar focus of the unit in a natural context. The Introduction texts, all of which are recorded on cassette, present language in various formats. These include newspaper and magazine excerpts, stories, transcripts of speeches, news broadcasts, radio shows, and other formats that students encounter in their day-to-day lives. In addition to presenting grammar in context, the Introduction serves to raise student motivation and provides an opportunity for incidental learning and lively classroom discussions. All Introductions are preceded by Questions to Consider, a feature that allows students to explore the topic that follows.

Grammar Charts

Grammar Charts follow each Introduction. These focus on the form and variety of the unit's target structure. As in all the ***Focus on Grammar*** texts, the charts are clear and easy to understand. These charts provide students with a clear visual reference for each new and reviewed structure.

Grammar Notes

The Grammar Notes that follow the charts focus on the meaning and use of the structure. Each note gives a clear explanation of the grammar point and is always followed by one or more examples. *Be careful!* notes alert students to common ESL/EFL errors. Subtleties of meaning and use are thoroughly explored in this advanced-level text. Cross-references to other related units and the Appendices make the book easy to use.

Focused Practice Exercises

These exercises follow the Grammar Notes. This section provides practice for all uses of the structures presented in the notes. Each Focused Practice section begins with a "for recognition only" exercise called Discover the Grammar. Here, the students are expected to recognize either the form of the structure or its meaning without having to produce any language. This activity raises awareness of the grammar as it builds confidence.

Following the Discover the Grammar activity are exercises that practice the grammar in a controlled, but still contextualized, environment. The exercises proceed from simpler to more complex. There is a large variety of exercise types including fill-in-the-blanks, matching, multiple choice, question and sentence formation, sentence combining, and error analysis through editing. As with the Introduction, students are exposed to many different written formats, including letters, journal entries, broadcast transcripts, essays, and newspaper and magazine articles. Topics are varied, providing rich and interesting contexts for meaningful practice. All Focused Practice exercises are suitable for self-study or homework. A complete Answer Key is provided at the end of this book.

Communication Practice Exercises

These exercises are intended for in-class use. The first exercise in this section is called Practice Listening. Having had exposure to and practice with the grammar in its written form, students now have the opportunity to check their aural comprehension. After listening to the tape (or hearing the teacher read the tapescript, which can be found in the Teacher's Manual), they complete a task that focuses on either the form or the meaning of the structure. It is suggested that students be allowed to hear the text as many times as they wish to complete the task successfully. In some units, an optional dictation follows the comprehension task to pave the way for the writing activity that is to follow later in the unit. In others, an open-ended discussion of the taped text is suggested to enhance the use of the tape.

Practice Listening is followed by a variety of activities that provide students with the opportunity to use the grammar in open-ended, interactive activities. Students work in pairs, small groups, or as a whole class, in discussions, role plays, and debates. Every unit gives students an opportunity to write an essay especially formulated to elicit practice of the unit's structures. Finally, a Picture Discussion in each unit enables students to apply their mastery of structure in a new and unrelated context. Many of the Picture Discussions are generated from reproductions of famous paintings esteemed throughout the world.

Review or SelfTest

At the conclusion of each of the eight parts, there is a review feature that can be used as a self-test. The exercises in this section test the form and use of the grammar content of the units in the part just concluded. Each test contains one exercise formatted in the same way as the Structure and Written Expression section of the TOEFL®.

From Grammar to Writing

This special feature of the advanced-level text in the ***Focus on Grammar*** series is designed to help students bridge the gap between writing in the ESL/EFL classroom and the less controlled writing that students may need to do outside of class, whether in everyday or academic settings. These optional units occur after the SelfTests and focus on such writing issues as the sentence; subject-verb agreement; parallelism; avoiding fragments, run-on sentences, and comma splices; punctuating adjective clauses; and capitalization and punctuation of direct and indirect speech. Although these writing issues are not solely ESL/EFL related, they are highly important to the ESL/EFL student who wants to write successfully.

In each From Grammar to Writing unit, the topic presented is related to the grammar content of the part just concluded. For example, the second writing unit on parallelism naturally and logically accompanies the gerund and infinitive part, since mixing gerunds and infinitives in a series is a common parallelism error.

Appendices

The twenty-five Appendices provide useful information, such as lists of common irregular verbs, common adjective-plus-preposition combinations, spelling rules, and lists of countries. The Appendices can help students do the unit exercises, act as a springboard for further classroom work, and serve as a reference source.

SUPPLEMENTARY COMPONENTS

The supplementary components of ***Focus on Grammar***—the Workbook, the Cassettes, and the Teacher's Manual—are all tightly keyed to the Student's Book, ensuring a wealth of practice and an opportunity to tailor the series to the needs of each individual classroom.

Cassettes

All of the Introduction texts and all of the Practice Listening exercises, as well as other selected exercises, are recorded on cassette. The symbol ▣ appears next to these activities. Listening scripts appear in the Teacher's Manual and may be used as an alternative way of presenting the listening activities.

Workbook

The Workbook accompanying ***Focus on Grammar: An Advanced Course for Reference and Practice*** provides a broad range of additional exercises appropriate for self-study of the target grammar of each unit in the Student's Book. Most of the exercises are fully contextualized with interesting and useful themes. There are also eight tests, one for each of the eight Student's Book parts. These tests have questions in the format of the Structure and Written Expression section of the TOEFL®. Besides reviewing the material in the Student's Book, these questions provide invaluable practice to those who are interested in taking this widely administered test.

Teacher's Manual

The Teacher's Manual, divided into three parts, contains a variety of suggestions and information to enrich the material in the Student's Book. The first part gives general suggestions for each section of a typical unit. The next part offers practical teaching suggestions and cultural information to accompany specific material in each unit. The Teacher's Manual offers suggestions to enhance students' vocabulary acquisition, both in presenting the meanings of new words and in aiding students to derive meaning from context on their own.

The Teacher's Manual also offers ready-to-use diagnostic and final tests for each of the eight parts of the Student's Book. In addition, a complete script of the cassette tapes is provided, as is an answer key for the diagnostic and final tests.

Software

The ***Focus on Grammar*** Software provides individualized practice based on each unit of the Student's Book. Fully contextualized and interactive, the activities broaden and extend practice of the grammatical structures in the reading, listening, and writing skill areas. The software includes grammar review, review tests, and all relevant reference material from the Student's Book. It can also be used alongside the *Longman Dictionary of American English* software.

Acknowledgments

Writing this book has been an excellent experience. I should really thank everyone I've ever met for inspiring me in the writing, especially my students over the years. Specifically, though, I want to express my appreciation and gratitude to the following folks:

Lyn McLean, who suggested me as the author for this book.

Joanne Dresner, who oversaw this project and inspired me all along the way. It wouldn't have been possible without her.

Jessica Miller, who provided encouragement and edited with a keen eye.

Allen Ascher, who was a driving force behind this project, kept it on track, and kept me laughing.

Lisa Hutchins, who guided the book through the production process with a good hand and good cheer.

Tom Finnegan, for perceptive and comprehensive copyediting.

Laura McCormick, for timely and helpful support on permissions.

The reviewers Laura T. LeDrean, Douglas Oliver, Ellen Rosenfield, Cynthia Wiseman, and Ramón Valenzuela, who made many valuable suggestions.

Special thanks are due to grammar consultant Sharon Hilles.

West Side, in all ways.

April, Becky, David, Diana, Jack, James, Jean, Jeff, Mackenzie, Marg, Rolleen, Thain, Zeya, and Mom. You were all there, and you're all here.

Above all, Joan Saslow. This is her book too.

Credits

Grateful acknowledgment is given for the following material:

"OUT, OUT—". From *The Poetry of Robert Frost*. Edited by Edward Connery Lathem. Henry Holt and Company.

Grateful acknowledgment is given to the following for providing photographs:

page 2	Steve Goldberg/MONKMEYER Press
page 12	Hugh Rogers/MONKMEYER Press
page 28	James L. Shaffer/Photo Edit
page 33	Spencer Grant/MONKMEYER Press
page 37	Brown Brothers
page 50	Paul Van Riel/Black Star
page 64	Claus Meyer/Black Star
page 76	AP/WIDE WORLD PHOTOS
page 99	Tony Freeman/Photo Edit
page 111	F. G. Taylor/Fortean Picture Library
page 119	Billy the Kid: Brown Brothers, Amelia Earhart: UPI/BETTMANN
page 120	UPI/BETTMANN
page 137	Joe Munroe/Photo Researchers, Inc
page 156	AP/WIDE WORLD PHOTOS
page 165	Rick Kopstein/MONKMEYER Press
page 175	AP/WIDE WORLD PHOTOS
page 177	Spencer Grant/Photo Researchers, Inc.
page 187	Laimute E. Druskis/Photo Researchers, Inc.
page 189	THE BETTMANN ARCHIVE
page 201	Mark N. Brultan/Photo Researchers, Inc.
page 203	J. Allen Cash/Photo Researchers, Inc.
page 252	Ursula Marious/Photo Researchers, Inc.
page 263	Tim Davis/Photo Researchers, Inc.

PART

V

Adverbials and Discourse Connectors

UNIT

12

Adverb Clauses

INTRODUCTION

Read and listen to the following interview from World Review *magazine.*

Questions to Consider

1. What effects does television have on people? Are they positive, negative, or both?
2. Can TV watching cause violence?
3. What other possible causes of violence and crime can you identify?

What Does the Expert Say?

Part I

World Review recently spoke with Dr. Krishna Das, a United Nations expert on crime and violence, particularly as they relate to the structure of families. Here is the first part of the interview.

World Review: Dr. Das, people used to say that violence was just an American problem, but today we see it **wherever we look.** Crime and violence aren't just American problems anymore, are they?

Das: No, not at all. Violence exists nearly everywhere in the world, and it's spreading; it's much more prevalent today **than it was even ten years ago. While it used to be fashionable to say it was strictly an American problem,** that is no longer true, **if it ever was true.**

WR: Why is this happening? What are the causes?

Das: Well, there are many complex causes. One, of course, is the shortage of jobs. **If people are employed in meaningful work activities,** they are much less likely to be involved in crime. Some say the easy availability of guns is another. And there's evidence to suggest that television promotes violence **because there's so much of it on TV** and **because certain people who watch it**—children especially—**apparently can't tell the difference between reality and the situations they see on TV programs.**

WR: Yes, we've heard a lot about the pervasive violence on TV, **although we could say the same thing about movies,** couldn't we? Aren't they just as violent as certain TV shows, if not more so?

Das: Yes, sometimes, but there are some key differences. For one thing, movies have gotten **so** expensive **that people are seeing fewer of them.** And **since we usually watch television in our own living rooms at home,** it seems like a "normal" rather than a special activity, part of the daily range of things we do. **If we see enough violent acts on TV,** we may become desensitized to the violence. But **when we go out to see a film,** we may unconsciously regard what we're seeing on the screen as somewhat out of the ordinary. **If we see someone shoot someone else in a film,** we tend on some level to recognize this as a kind of "performance" as we would a theatrical play. Another reason that movies contribute less to violence is that the film ratings establish some control over what children can see—**provided that they are enforced.**

WR: OK. But **even if it's true that TV watching causes violence,** what can we do about it?

Das: I think we will have to accept the notion that we can't have total freedom in everything. You may remember that in the early nineties, the U.S. attorney general suggested that TV networks in America must "clean up their act" and that, **unless they do it themselves,** the government will have do to it for them.

WR: What would that mean—cleaning up their act?

Das: A clearly defined code of decency would have to be established for television programs. Networks and producers would have to agree not to show material that violated this code, at least during the hours of the day when children would be likly to be watching. But that leads me to a second major cause of societal violence today: the breakdown of family structure. Actually, I've run out of time. We'll have to save the discussion of that for the next interview.

ADVERB CLAUSES*

CLAUSE OF REASON
Television violence may influence crime **because there is so much violent behavior on TV.**

CLAUSE OF CONTRAST
We've heard a lot about violence on TV, **although we could say the same thing about movies.**

CLAUSE OF CONDITION
If we see enough violent acts on TV, we may become desensitized to violence.

CLAUSE OF TIME
When we go out to see a film, we regard it as a special activity.

CLAUSE OF PLACE
Today we see violence **wherever we look.**

CLAUSE OF COMPARISON
Violence is much more prevalent today **than it was even ten years ago.**

CLAUSE OF RESULT
Movies have gotten **so** expensive **that people are seeing fewer of them.**

*Adverb clauses of manner with *as if* and *as though* are discussed in Unit 20.

Grammar Notes

1. A clause is a group of words that contains at least a subject and its verb. Clauses can be either independent or dependent. Independent clauses (also called main clauses) can stand alone as complete sentences. They do not need another clause to be fully understood. Dependent clauses (also called subordinate clauses), on the other hand, do need another clause to be fully understood.

INDEPENDENT CLAUSE

Violence is increasing today

DEPENDENT CLAUSE

because children watch too much TV.

2. Adverb clauses are dependent clauses that answer questions such as *why, where, how,* or *when* in the same way that single adverbs do.

Wherever there are gangs, there is violence. (answers the question "Where is there violence?")

Speakers and writers use adverb clauses to combine thoughts and show connections between ideas. They also use them to vary their writing style. Compare these two ways to convey an idea.

Television violence may promote crime. The reason for this is that there is a lot of violence on TV. (two sentences)
Television violence may promote crime because there is a lot of violence on TV. (one sentence made up by combining an independent clause and a dependent adverb clause)

Sentences made up of an independent clause and a dependent clause introduced by a subordinating conjunction are called complex sentences. In a complex sentence the main idea is usually in the independent clause.

3. Following are seven important types of adverb clauses, listed with the subordinating conjunctions and expressions that can introduce each type of clause (see Appendix 21 on page A24 for a more complete list of subordinating conjunctions):

a. Adverb clauses of reason: introduced by *because, since, on account of the fact that.* These clauses answer the question "why?"

Since we watch TV at home, we tend to regard it as a "normal" activity.
Some teenagers get into crime **on account of the fact that they don't have enough to do.**

b. Adverb clauses of contrast: introduced by *although, though, even though, while, in spite of the fact that.* These clauses present a contrast with the idea expressed in the independent clause.

TV has some very serious negative qualities, **though it has some positive qualities as well.**
In spite of the fact that there have been many protests, there is still a lot of violence on TV.

c. Adverb clauses of condition: introduced by *if, unless, in case, provided (that).* These clauses answer the question "under what condition?"

If children watch too much TV, they may lose the ability to distinguish fantasy from reality.
TV violence won't be reduced **unless viewers protest.**

d. Adverb clauses of time: introduced by *when, whenever, before, after, as, as soon as, while, since, until.* These clauses answer the question "when?"

We need to recognize the problem **before we can solve it.**
When we reduce the amount of TV violence, we will begin to see a decline in violent crime.

(continued on next page)

e. Adverb clauses of place: introduced by *where, wherever*. These clauses answer the question "where?"

We need to place the blame **where it belongs.**
Wherever there are gangs, there is violence.

f. Adverb clauses of comparison: introduced by *than, as much as, as many as*. These clauses make comparisons of quantity.

There is far more gang activity today **than there was even ten years ago.**
Today there are probably **as many** violent crimes committed in a month **as there used to be in a year.**

g. Adverb clauses of result: introduced by *so (that)* or containing the expressions *so* + adjective + *that* or *such* + noun phrase + *that*. These clauses present the result of a situation stated in the independent clause.

The networks will have to clean up their act **so (that) the government won't have to do it for them.**
Crime is increasing **so** fast **that we will have to build more prisons to hold the criminals.**
Some children have **such** terrifying experiences at school **that they refuse to go.**

4. Except for clauses of comparison and result, most adverb clauses can come either before or after the independent clause. When the adverb clause comes first, we place a comma after it. When the adverb clause comes second, we generally do not place a comma before it.

Because there is so much violence on TV, many people want more government control of programming.
Many people want more government control of programming **because there is so much violence on TV.**

We place a comma before a dependent clause, however, if the dependent clause sets up a contrast.

We can deal with the problem of violence**, though it won't be easy.**

5. Unlike the other adverb clauses, adverb clauses of comparison and result cannot normally be moved. This is because their meaning is linked to or dependent on a particular element in the independent clause.

There is far **more** gang activity today
than there was even ten years ago.

Today there are probably **as many** violent crimes committed in a month
as there used to be in a year.

Crime is increasing **so** fast
that we will have to build more prisons to hold the criminals.

Some children have **such** terrifying experiences at school
that they refuse to go.

Be careful! Note the difference between *so* and *such*. *So* occurs before an adjective or adverb with no following noun. *Such* occurs before a noun or noun phrase.

so fast
so incredibly fast
such terrifying experiences
such a happy couple

FOCUSED PRACTICE

1. Discover the Grammar

In each of the following sentences, underline the dependent clause once and the independent clause twice.

1. Police confiscate illegal weapons wherever they find them.
2. We won't be able to correct the problem of violence unless we treat its underlying causes.
3. Some cartoons contain as much violence as R-rated movies do.
4. Though the drug problem has worsened, there are some positive signs.
5. Some parents curtail their children's TV watching because they think it encourages passivity.
6. There are so few programs of quality on television that some people have gotten rid of their TV sets.
7. Whenever there is an economic downturn, there is a corresponding increase in crime.

2. Why Sports?

Read the essay, which contains twelve adverb clauses. Underline all of the adverb clauses. Determine the role each clause plays in the sentence. Write **where, when, why,** *or* **under what condition** *above the clauses that answer those questions. Write* **result, comparison,** *or* **contrast** *above the clauses that present results, comparisons, or contrasts.*

WHY SPORTS?

by Jamal Jefferson

A lot of people are criticizing school sports these days. Some say there's too much emphasis on football and basketball and not enough on education. Others say the idea of the scholar-athlete is a joke. Still others say sports are a way of encouraging violence. I think they're all wrong. If anything, school sports help prevent violence, not encourage it. Why do I think sports are a positive force?

For one thing, sports are positive *why* because they give students opportunities to be involved in something. Every day on TV we hear that violence is increasing. I think a lot of people get involved in crime on account of the fact that they don't have enough to do to keep themselves busy. After two or three hours of basketball, baseball, or any other kind of sports practice, you're so tired that it's hard to commit a violent act.

Second, sports teach people a lot of worthwhile things, especially at the high school level. By playing on a team, students learn to get along and work with others. When their team wins, they learn how to be good winners; when their team loses, they find out they have to struggle to improve. They discover that winning a few and losing a few are part of the normal ups and downs of life. Also, there's no doubt that students improve their physical condition by participating in sports.

Finally, sports are positive because they give some students, especially poor ones, an opportunity to get out of a difficult situation and improve their chances for a successful life. If a young basketball player from a poor village in Nigeria can get a scholarship to play for, say, UCLA, he will have a chance to get an education and make his life better than it ever was. If a young woman coming from a ghetto is accepted on the University of Missouri swim team, she'll have the chance to permanently leave that ghetto and be successful wherever she goes. In spite of the fact that some school sporting programs have deficiencies that need to be ironed out, their benefits outweigh their disadvantages. I should know because I'm one of those students. School sports must stay.

3. Crime Prevention

A panel of experts has been investigating the causes of crime. Write their conclusions by combining each of the following pairs of sentences into one sentence with a dependent clause and an independent clause. Place the idea that seems more important in the independent clause. Use the indicated subordinating conjunctions. Do not add words.

1. We can begin to solve the crime problem. We must look at the underlying causes of violence. (before)

   Before we can begin to solve the crime problem, we must look at the underlying causes of violence.

2. Many citizens support gun control. They believe that the easy availability of guns is a key ingredient in violent crime. (because) ______________________________

   ____

3. Many citizens do not support gun control. They recognize that guns are part of the crime problem. (although) ______________________________

   ____

4. Teenagers have meaningful activities. They are likely to get involved in crime. (unless)

   ____

   ____

5. There is potential danger. We go. (wherever) ______________________________

   ____

6. Criminals commit three serious crimes. They will be sent to life in prison without possibility of parole. (if)

   ____

   ____

7. The Brady Law to control handguns was finally passed. Its supporters had lobbied for years for its passage. (after) ______________________________

   ____

8. Politicians argue about the war on drugs. The drug problem continues to grow. (while)

   ____

   ____

4. Traffic Court

Stan Everly was involved in an automobile accident and is explaining his side of the story to the judge of the traffic court. Fill in the blanks in their conversation, using the subordinating conjunctions and expressions from the box to complete the dependent clauses.

as much . . . as	in spite of the fact that
more . . . than	on account of the fact that
so . . . that	such . . . that
if	

Judge: Well, Mr. Everly, your description of the accident is ____so____ confusingly written ____that____ (1.) I'm not sure I understand it. Tell me in your own words what happened.

Everly: Well, your honor, I had just received a telephone call from the nurse at my daughter's school. I was speeding ________ (2.) she'd been hurt in an accident, and I was frantic to get there.

Judge: OK. What happened next?

Everly: Well, I sideswiped that parked car, and I was in ________ a hurry ________ (3.) I didn't have time to leave a note on the driver's windshield.

Judge: What? This is ________ serious ________ (4.) I thought. You left the scene of the accident without notifying the driver of the other car?

Everly: Yes, your honor.

Judge: Well, Mr. Everly, a crime is a crime, and I don't have ________ patience with these kinds of cases ________ (5.) I used to. ________ (6.) there were extenuating circumstances, I can't dismiss these charges. I'm fining you $150. ________ (7.) something like this happens again, I'll revoke your license.

5. Editing

Each of the following sentences contains an error in the dependent clause, either in structure or in logical word choice. Rewrite each sentence, correcting the error.

1. We won't make a dent in crime until identify the root causes of violence.

   We won't make a dent in crime until we identify the root causes of violence.

2. The prison escapee was driving such rapidly that he lost control of the car and was apprehended.

   ____

(continued on next page)

3. If get enough attention from their parents, children probably won't turn to crime.

____

4. Some children watch so a lot of television that they have trouble telling reality from fantasy.

____

5. The sheriff's office has put more agents on the streets in case there being additional trouble.

____

6. Provided their governments to appropriate enough money, nations everywhere can gain headway against crime.

____

7. Today there is more awareness about the underlying causes of violence than there be in the past.

____

8. Many juvenile criminals today receive light sentences although commit serious crimes.

____

9. Today there isn't as much abuse of certain drugs than there used to be. That's a positive sign.

____

10. In spite of he had exhibited good behavior, the prisoner was denied parole.

____

COMMUNICATION PRACTICE

6. Practice Listening

Bradley Freeman and Jennifer Strand are having a debate on gun control. Listen to their conversation on the tape.

Now listen to certain of the sentences again. Circle the letter of the choice which correctly explains the meaning of each sentence you hear.

1. (a.) Jennifer thinks people are likely to use guns if they have them.
   b. Jennifer thinks people probably won't use guns even if they have them.
2. a. According to Bradley, people don't die because other people have guns.
   b. According to Bradley, people die because other people have guns.

3. a. Bradley thinks law-abiding citizens die because they have guns.
   b. Bradley thinks law-abiding citizens die because a lot of criminals don't get punished.
4. a. Jennifer thinks a person who has a gun probably won't shoot anybody.
   b. Jennifer thinks that in any situation where a person has a gun, it is more likely that someone will be shot.
5. a. Bradley thinks it's true that if we outlaw guns, outlaws will still be able to get them.
   b. Bradley thinks it's true that if we outlaw guns, outlaws won't be able to get them.
6. a. Jennifer thinks outlawing guns is a criminal act.
   b. Jennifer doesn't think outlawing guns is a criminal act.
7. a. According to Jennifer, getting rid of guns won't change the attitude toward violence.
   b. According to Jennifer, getting rid of guns will change the attitude toward violence.
8. a. Bradley thinks we must change the attitude toward punishment before we can change the attitude toward violence.
   b. Bradley thinks we must change the attitude toward violence before we can change the attitude toward punishment.
9. a. According to Bradley, we need to build more prisons to cause violence to decline.
   b. According to Bradley, building more prisons won't cause violence to decline.
10. a. Jennifer thinks incarceration of violent criminals is the real answer to the problem.
    b. Jennifer doesn't think incarceration of violent criminals is the real answer to the problem.

7. Small Group Discussion

Combine each of the following ideas with a dependent clause to express your own ideas. Then choose one of the topics to discuss with the other members of your group.

1. We won't get control of the crime problem.
   We won't get control of the crime problem until we identify the real causes of violence.
   ____
2. We can provide jobs for everyone.
   ____
3. Parents should not leave their children home alone.
   ____
4. The number of gun-related deaths has increased a great deal in the last decade.
   ____

(continued on next page)

5. Parents need to limit their children's television viewing.

____

6. Some people have proposed legalization of drugs as a solution to the crime problem.

____

8. Role Play in Pairs

Work with a partner. Look at the four illustrations. Choose one situation and role-play the parts of the two people pictured. Use as many of the words and expressions from the box as you can.

because	as many as	in spite of the fact that
since	than	if
on account of the fact that	so . . . that	unless
although	such . . . that	in case
though	so (that)	provided (that)
as much as	even though	when
whenever	before	after
as	as soon as	while
until	where	wherever

9. Essay

Choose one of the following clauses and begin a short essay with it.

Clause 1. Because guns are a key ingredient in the escalation of violence all over the world, . . .
Clause 2. Although guns are a key ingredient in the escalation of violence all over the world, . . .
Clause 3. Because watching television is essentially a passive activity, . . .
Clause 4. Because drugs are so pervasive in today's society, . . .

10. Picture Discussion

Form two teams. Make a list of the positive and negative effects of team sports. Then, have a debate about this issue, with one team taking the positive side and the other taking the negative side.

UNIT 13

Adverbials: Viewpoint, Focus, and Negative

INTRODUCTION

Read and listen to the second half of the interview with Dr. Krishna Das.

Questions to Consider

1. Do you think that family structure is declining?
2. Do you think a decline in family structure can promote violence?
3. Would providing people with fewer work hours and more leisure time help reduce violence and crime?

What Does the Expert Say?

Part II

World Review: When we left off the last interview, Dr. Das, you were about to talk about the breakdown of family structure as a factor in violence.

Das: Yes. As I was saying, restricting the amount of violence shown on TV is only the beginning. The real key is to strengthen the role of parents. They should be able to limit the amount of television their children watch and to control what they see. They even need to be able to say to their children, "We're not watching any TV **at all** this evening."

But far more important is their need **simply** to be with their children more. **Even** in many well-off families, both parents have to work just to make ends meet. **Sadly,** because of this, many parents find it difficult or impossible to have close involvement with their children. **Seldom** do they have enough time for all the things they want and need to do. When working parents come home from work, they are usually tired; **rarely** do they have enough energy to play with their children, read to them, that sort of thing. They often use TV as a babysitter, **unfortunately.** This is understandable because someone has to do the chores. But what happens? They put the children in front of the television set, **perhaps** not **even** supervising what they are watching.

WR: But this is a colossal problem, isn't it? How can we address it?

Das: Yes, it's **certainly** a difficult issue, though solving it is not impossible. There are a number of things that could be done for starters. **At the top of the list** is the need for workplace day care, where parents could see their young children periodically during the workday. Day care personnel would be licensed, supervised professionals who would guide the children in meaningful activities in a caring environment. **Second on the list** is the need to reduce the workweek so that parents would have more time to spend with their children and with each other. **Maybe** we could cut it down to thirty-five or thirty-two hours. And **not only** should we reduce the workweek, but we should also encourage and expand the use of flextime.

WR: How would flextime help the situation?

Das: By allowing employees to work shifts that reflect the demands of their families' schedules so that one parent could always be available when children need care. In these ways, **perhaps,** we would give people some crucial extra time to spend with their families. It could help tremendously.

WR: This all sounds good, but wouldn't it take a lot of money?

Das: Clearly, but that seems a small price to pay. We must strengthen the family structure. **Only** then will we be able to reduce the level of crime and violence.

WR: Well, Dr. Das, you've provided much food for thought. Thank you for your comments. **Perhaps** we can discuss other solutions in a future interview.

Das: Yes, thank you. I would like that.

ADVERBIALS: VIEWPOINT, FOCUS, AND NEGATIVE

VIEWPOINT ADVERBS
Fortunately, quality day care is available.
Crime is **certainly** a serious problem.
Family structure has declined, **clearly.**
Perhaps limiting TV watching will help.
Maybe violent crime will be reduced.

FOCUS ADVERBS
The Millers have **only** one child.
They **only** want the best for her.
They have saved **almost** $20,000.
They have **even** made arrangements for her admission to college.
They **just** want her to be happy.

NEGATIVE ADVERBS
Rarely has the situation been this dangerous.
Seldom do they supervise their children.
Never before have crime levels been so high.

Grammar Notes

1. Viewpoint adverbs give the speaker or writer's viewpoint or comment about the statement made, modifying entire sentences rather than elements within them. They include *fortunately, unfortunately, clearly, obviously, certainly, luckily, surely, evidently, frankly, actually, perhaps,* and *maybe*. Note the difference in the meaning of *sadly* in the following sentences.

   The mother reacted **sadly** to the news.
   Sadly, she was unable to do anything to help.

   The adverb *sadly* in the first sentence modifies *reacted*, showing the manner in which the mother reacted to the news. The word *sadly* in the second sentence is a viewpoint adverb which shows the speaker or writer's comment about the situation.

   Placement: Except for *maybe* and *perhaps,* viewpoint adverbs can appear at the beginning of a sentence, in its middle, or at the end. When they appear at the beginning of the sentence, they often have a comma separating them from the rest of the sentence. When they appear at the end of the sentence, they are always preceded by a comma. If they appear in the middle, they are always close to the verb and are usually enclosed in commas when they precede the verb. In general, writers use the comma when they want to separate the viewpoint adverb from the rest of the sentence.

   Fortunately, use of certain drugs is declining.
   Use of certain drugs is declining**, fortunately.**
   Use of certain drugs is **fortunately** declining.
   Use of certain drugs**, fortunately,** is declining.

   Usage note: The word *hopefully* is often used as a viewpoint adverb meaning "it is to be hoped that." However, some speakers and writers object to its use.

2. Focus adverbs include *only, just, even, almost, merely, really,* and *simply.* Like viewpoint adverbs, they are flexible words that can appear in many places in a sentence. In writing and in formal speaking, we place focus adverbs just before or after words or phrases that we want to focus on specifically. The following examples show how strongly focus adverbs affect meaning.

   The Millers have **only** one child. The Millers have one child **only.** (Focus on **one** or **one child** = She is all the children they have.)
   They want **only** the best for her. (Focus on **the best** = This is all they want.)

   I **almost** called the police. (Focus on **called** = I was about to call but changed my mind.)
   I made **almost** fifty calls yesterday. (Focus on **fifty** or **fifty calls** = I made nearly fifty calls yesterday.)

   Even Ms. Smith signed the petition. (Focus on **Ms. Smith** = She would not be expected to sign it.)
   Ms. Smith **even** signed the petition. (Focus on **signed** = It was one of many things that she did.)

   Placement: In informal speech and writing, the adverbs *only* and *just* usually occur before the verb. In speaking the meaning is made clear through stress and intonation:

   I ONLY asked Mr. Green for his opinion. (Strong stress on **only** = That's all that I did.)
   I ONLY asked MR. GREEN for his opinion. (Strong stress on **only** and **Mr. Green** = Mr. Green is the only person I asked.)
   I ONLY asked Mr. Green for his OPINION. (Strong stress on **only** and **opinion** = I asked him for his opinion, not his support.)

3. Negative adverbials include *never, rarely, seldom, scarcely, not only, only then, neither, hardly, little, on no account.* They often occur in the same position as frequency adverbs. Because negative adverbials are already negative, the verb in the sentence doesn't need the word *not.*

   Parents **rarely** have much energy after work.

   Placement: For emphasis, negative adverbs are sometimes placed at the

(continued on next page)

beginning of a sentence, especially in writing or more formal speech. When they come at the beginning, they force the subject and auxiliary to invert.

Seldom have I been so disappointed.
Hardly had we left when the car quit.
Not only is she a good parent, but she is also a good daughter.
Only then will we be able to solve the problem.

In sentences in simple present or simple past, subject-auxiliary inversion forces the appearance of the auxiliary *do/does/did.*

Rarely do parents have much energy after work.

Placing negative adverbials at the beginning of the sentence sounds somewhat formal to most native speakers and is less common in conversation than in writing.

4. Like the negative adverbials, certain other adverbials can be placed at the beginning of a sentence, particularly in descriptive writing. When they are, the subject and verb are inverted if the subject is a noun.

At the top of the list is the need for governments to provide day care in the workplace.
Second on the list is the need to reduce the workweek.

In both formal and informal English, this type of inversion is common if the sentence begins with *here* or *there* and a noun follows.

Here are your **books.** Run and catch the bus!
There goes the **bus!** You missed it.

Be careful! Inversion after *here* and *there* occurs only when the subject is a noun. If the subject is a pronoun, the word order is normal.

Here **they are.**
There **it goes.**

5. Be careful! The adverbial *at all* occurs only in negative and interrogative sentences. It is often used with the indefinite pronouns. It also never begins a sentence.

Is there **anything** we can do **at all?**
Is there **anything at all** we can do?
I don't like television **at all.**

FOCUSED PRACTICE

1. Discover the Grammar

Part 1 *The Martins took a family trip to Disneyland. Circle the focus adverb in each of the following statements about their excursion. Note that the word the adverb focuses on is boxed.*

1. Jim and Helen Martin and their four children took a trip to Disneyland. They had been saving money for (almost) [two] years.
2. They left for the airport. The traffic was heavy, and they almost [missed] the plane.
3. The children were keyed up about the trip. Even seventeen-year-old [Nancy] was excited.
4. They arrived at the park. Eight-year-old Michael had only [ten dollars] to spend on souvenirs.

5. Only [Eric] had enough money to buy what he wanted.
6. Nancy was in a good mood. She even [lent] her brother Michael twenty dollars.
7. Jim and Helen wanted to watch the parades. The children only [wanted] to go on the rides.
8. Michael wanted to go on only [one] ride: Space Mountain.
9. Sam and Eric, the thirteen-year-old twins, just [wanted] to visit the arcades.
10. At the end of the day, the Martins had just [three] dollars left.

Part 2 *Look again at some sentences adapted from the interview with Dr. Das. Find and circle fourteen viewpoint, focus, or negative adverbials. One sentence has two adverbials.*

1. But that's (only) the beginning.
2. You can watch just one hour of TV this evening.
3. But far more important is their need simply to be with their children.
4. Even in many well-off families in the United States, both parents have to work just to make ends meet.
5. Sadly, many parents find it difficult or impossible to develop close involvement with their children.
6. Seldom do they have enough time for all the things they want and need to do.
7. Rarely do they have enough energy to play with their children, read to them, that sort of thing.
8. They often use TV as a babysitter, unfortunately.
9. Yes, it's certainly a difficult issue.
10. Not only should we reduce the workweek, but we should also encourage and expand the concept of flextime.
11. Instead of requiring everyone to work from nine to five only, we ought to try to accommodate people's individual situations.
12. Clearly, but that seems a small price to pay.
13. Only then will we be able to reduce the level of crime and violence.

2. Talking to Parents

Dr. Krishna Das is talking with a group of parents who want to know about violence and what they might do about it. Combine the ideas in the following pairs of sentences to create his statements to the parents. Use a viewpoint adverb in each case. Note that a viewpoint adverb can appear in at least three places in a sentence. Write three sentences for each numbered item.

1. Children should not have to go to school in constant fear about crime. That is clear.

Clearly, children should not have to go to school in constant fear about crime.

Children should clearly not have to go to school in constant fear about crime.

Children should not have to go to school in constant fear about crime, clearly.

(continued on next page)

2. Violence has increased in public schools. This is an unfortunate development.

____

____

____

3. Some parents are able to spend a great deal of time with their children. This is a lucky situation.

____

____

____

4. We must be willing to make some sacrifices. I am sure of this.

____

____

____

5. Some young people manage to survive unhappy childhoods. This is fortunate.

____

____

____

6. Some schools have no policies on bringing guns to campus. That is evident.

____

____

____

7. It is important to place limits on your children's behavior. I am being frank.

____

____

____

3. Talking to a Teenager

Shari and Jonathan Hughes are having a discussion with their daughter Alison, who violated her curfew last night. Fill in the blanks in their conversation, using the focus adverbs given. Consider the context carefully in deciding where the focus adverbs should be placed.

Shari: Alison, it was 2 A.M. when you got home last night. ___We were really___ (1. (Really, we were / We were really)) worried. ______________ (2. (Almost I got up and called / I almost got up and called)) the police, but your father persuaded me to stay in bed. Who were you out with, and what were you doing?

Alison: I was with Jerry at a restaurant. ______________ (3. (Only we were talking / We were only talking)) and drinking coffee. We weren't doing anything bad. I ______________ (4. (just guess we lost / guess we just lost)) track of time.

Jonathan: But why didn't you ______________________ us you'd be late?
5. (simply call and tell / call and tell simply)
______________________ knows enough to do that.
6. (Your little brother even / Even your little brother)

Alison: I did. I ______________________ ten times, but the line was busy.
7. (almost called / called almost)

Shari: Busy? The phone didn't ring once, and it wasn't off the hook.

Alison: Well, uh . . .

Jonathan: Alison, we can't monitor your every move. You're old enough now to make some of your own decisions. I ______________________ know the difference between right and
8. (just hope you / hope you just)
wrong. There are going to be times when ______________________ decide that.
9. (only you can / you can only)
In this case, I don't know if ______________________ be punished. We'd like to
10. (even you should / you should even)
be able to trust you.

Alison: You can, Dad, you can.

4. Families

Read the following statements about families. Then rewrite them, beginning each sentence with the negative adverbial provided.

1. Fathers gain custody of the children in divorce cases. (Rarely)
   Rarely do fathers gain custody of the children in divorce cases.
2. Families eat meals together. (All too seldom)
   ____
3. Domestic violence can be ignored. (On no account)
   ____
4. Young people should start paying their own bills. They will begin to truly appreciate their parents. (Only then)
   ____
5. A teenager knows about how difficult it is to be a parent. (Little)
   ____
6. They understand the need for discipline. (Hardly ever)
   ____

5. Editing

Find and correct the ten errors in adverbials in the following letter.

April15

Dear Mom,

I'm sitting in the train station, waiting for the 5:25 to come along, so ~~just I~~ I just thought I'd drop you a quick note.

Tax day is over with, at long last! Almost we didn't get our taxes done on time, but Jonathan and I stayed up until midnight last night, and I mailed the forms this afternoon. I hate income taxes! Only once in the last ten years we have gotten a refund, and this time the tax return was so complicated that Jonathan got even upset, and you know how calm he is.

Besides that, we've been having a few problems with Alison. It's probably nothing more serious than teenage rebellion, but whenever we try to lay down the law, she gets defensive. Rarely if ever she takes criticism well. The other night she and her boyfriend stayed out until 2:00 A.M.—this was the second time in two weeks—and when we asked her what they'd been doing she said, "Only we were talking and listening to dance music at the Teen Club. Why can't you leave me alone?" Then she stomped out of the room. Fortunately, Karen and Kenny have been behaving like angels—but they're not teenagers yet!

Meanwhile, Alison's school has started a new open-campus policy. Students can leave the campus whenever they don't have a class. Even they don't have to tell the school office where they're going and when they'll be back. Jonathan and I approve of that policy at all. School is for studying and learning, not for socializing. Little those school officials realize how much trouble teenagers can get into whenever they're roaming around unsupervised.

Well, here the train comes. I'll sign off now. Write soon.

Love,
Shari

COMMUNICATION PRACTICE

6. Practice Listening 1

Janet Robertson, a member of a newspaper editorial staff, is interviewing Dr. Krishna Das about Bob Brown, a teenager who was arrested for shoplifting. Listen to their conversation on the tape. Then listen again, marking the following statements true (T) *or false* (F), *based on what you hear.*

__T__ 1. Dr. Das can be easily understood when he speaks about juvenile delinquency.

_____ 2. Robertson thinks that jail is an appropriate punishment for shoplifting.

_____ 3. Dr. Das feels that Bob's arrest will have a good effect on him.

_____ 4. Bob's mother felt unhappy when he was arrested.

_____ 5. Bob's mother doesn't think his arrest will have a good effect.

_____ 6. Robertson is certain that Bob can be rehabilitated.

_____ 7. Dr. Das says that Bob's shoplifting was no mistake.

_____ 8. Dr. Das says that Bob will happily serve his sentence.

_____ 9. Robertson is reconsidering her opinion about the case.

7. Tape Discussion

Are people benefited by punishment?

8. Practice Listening 2

Listen to the tape. Pay close attention to the speakers' stress and intonation. Circle the letter of the sentence that explains the meaning of the sentence you hear.

1. (a.) That's all I asked her to do.
   b. That's all I asked her to vacuum.
2. a. That's all I asked Alison to do.
   b. Alison was the only person I asked.
3. a. I didn't ask her to do anything else to the living room.
   b. I didn't ask anyone else to vacuum the living room.

(continued on next page)

4. a. Jerry is the only person Alison dates.

   b. Alison doesn't go steady with Jerry.

5. a. Jerry is the only person Alison dates.

   b. Alison doesn't go steady with Jerry.

6. a. All I want to do is talk.

   b. You're the only person I want to talk to.

7. a. All I want to do is talk.

   b. You're the only person I want to talk to.

8. a. It's only tonight that I want to talk to you.

   b. It's only you that I want to talk to tonight.

9. a. Jerry is the only person Alison is friends with.

   b. That's all Alison and Jerry are—friends.

10. a. Jerry is the only person Alison is friends with.

    b. That's all Alison and Jerry are—friends.

9. Small Group Discussion

Work in small groups to role-play one or more of the following situations. Try to incorporate some of the adverbs in the box into your role play.

fortunately	actually	even	rarely
unfortunately	almost	only	never

1. You and your spouse both have full-time jobs, but you can't afford day care. You are talking with each other about a solution to the problem.

   Example:
   Spouse 1: Honey, what do you think we ought to do about day care for the kids?
   Spouse 2: Well, I've got a plan, and it might **actually** work. Would your boss let you have one of the weekdays off if you worked on Saturday?
   Spouse 1: I don't know. Why?
   Spouse 2: We could set up an all-day play group for the small kids in the neighborhood. We'd **only** need four other sets of parents. . . .

2. You are a parent and you believe that requiring all students to wear uniforms in schools would improve the school climate. You are trying to convince the school board to accept your idea.
3. Children need to have a sense that their parents care about them. You have just had a terrible argument with your teenage daughter, and she told you that you're always too busy to pay any attention to her. You are talking with her.
4. Your teenage son is "running with a bad crowd." You are talking with him about it.
5. Violence in some schools has become so serious that many children do not feel safe. You are a high school principal and are talking with a group of parents about the issue.
6. Truancy in schools has become more and more widespread. Your ten-year-old daughter has been caught by the truancy officer, and you are talking with her about the problem.

10. Essay

Choose one of the following topics and write an essay of three or four paragraphs about it.

Topic 1. To reverse the breakdown of family structure, we . . .
Topic 2. To communicate better within our families, we . . .
Topic 3. To reduce violence in society, we . . .
Topic 4. Flextime should be encouraged.
Topic 5. The day care system should be vastly expanded.

11. Picture Discussion

Look at this picture of a day care center and consider the impact of day care on society. Then, in groups of four or five, participate in a panel discussion for a TV news program with each person taking one of the following roles: day care administrator, working parent whose child is in the day care center, parent opposed to day care, child psychologist, and moderator.

UNIT

14

Other Discourse Connectors

INTRODUCTION

Read and listen to this essay about the automobile in the modern world.

Questions to Consider

1. Do you think that the automobile has exerted negative as well as positive influences on society? Explain your viewpoint.
2. Suppose it were determined that the only way to curb pollution and solve other car-related problems would be to sharply curtail, if not ban, car use. Would you give up your car?

WOULD YOU GIVE UP YOUR CAR?

by Helen Moreaux

On October 1, 1908, Henry Ford introduced the Model T to the world, setting in motion the process of making the car available "to the multitude." The rest is history. Ford, of course, didn't invent the car, but he did popularize it. **In fact,** today cars are *so* popular and define our world so much that it's worth taking a look at what they have done for us and to us. **Besides** looking at the car's effects, we can also speculate on what we can do to control the car instead of letting it control us.

First, cars have vastly increased our mobility. A thirty-mile trip that in the nineteenth century would have taken two days by horse and carriage or three or four days on foot can today be made in an hour or less. **Along with** mobility, **however,** comes stress. The car is available to nearly everyone, and monstrous traffic jams are created **as a result.** We get nervous or angry if the car ahead of us isn't moving or if someone cuts in front of us. This causes stress, and too much stress can even kill.

Second, cars have allowed people the freedom to live far from their workplaces. And when we go shopping, we don't have to buy enough supplies to last a month or two, **for** it's easy just to stop at the supermarket on the way home to get food for supper. **On the other hand,** the car has its negatives. **Despite** giving us freedom, it has also contributed to the decline of community. Instead of taking public transportation to work and interacting with other passengers, many of us ride alone in our autos. **Moreover,** we used to buy things at local stores where we knew the proprietors,

but today we largely trade with strangers at vast, impersonal commercial centers. **In addition,** modern neighborhoods are hardly neighborhoods in the old sense of a place where people come into daily contact with each other; **instead,** they are locations accessible above all to the automobile and are **thus** controlled by it. **Consequently,** the concept of the neighborhood has been weakened.

Finally, we know the car industry has created jobs, industries, and companies: rubber, steel, electronics. Jobs aren't everything, **though;** there is a downside. **For one thing,** the economy is dependent on the automobile, perhaps too dependent. In recent years, **for example,** certain car manufacturers have moved their factories for increased profits. **However,** the towns housing the original factories have been devastated by increased unemployment. **And** we must not forget that, in addition to dominating the economy, the automobile is the source of much air pollution.

Clearly, the effect of the car on human society has been momentous. But we can't now "uninvent" cars or abolish them. They are far too necessary and beneficial to our world. **Nevertheless,** we must get control of the car, develop new fuel sources, and reduce air pollution. These are the challenges that face us.

Other Discourse Connectors

COORDINATING CONJUNCTIONS

It used to be common to buy things at neighborhood stores, **but** now we trade at vast, impersonal shopping malls.
The automobile provides jobs, **and** it gives us mobility.
We can take the train, **or** we can drive.
I was spending three hours a day commuting in my car, **so** I switched to the train.

TRANSITIONS

Ford, of course, didn't invent the car. **However,** he probably did more than anyone else to popularize it.
Oil and gasoline won't last forever. **Therefore,** we will have to develop new fuel sources.
In addition to dominating the economy, cars are the source of much air pollution.

Grammar Notes

1. Discourse connectors are words and expressions that tie together the ideas in a piece of writing or in speech. They join ideas both within sentences and between sentences or larger stretches of text.

   joins ideas within complex sentence
   He's a terrible driver **even though** he's had a license for years.

   joins ideas between sentences
   Ford didn't invent the car. **However,** he probably did more than anyone else to popularize it.

   Two important types of discourse connectors are coordinating conjunctions and transitions.

2. The coordinating conjunctions (*and, but, or, nor, for, so,* and *yet*) connect ideas within sentences, joining two independent clauses. Sentences made up of two or more independent clauses joined by a coordinating conjunction are called compound sentences.

   On our vacation we drove our car, **and** we also traveled by bicycle. (**And** adds information.)
   Cars give us freedom, **but** they also cause stress. (**But** presents a contrast.)
   You can drive your car, **or** you can take the bus. (**Or** adds information.)
   Catherine doesn't like taking the subway, **nor** do I. (**Nor** adds information.)
   Nick's driver's license was revoked, **for** he had been convicted of drunk driving. (**For** presents a cause.)
   Catherine's automobile broke down, **so** she had to use public transportation. (**So** presents an effect.)
   I'm glad that James has his driver's license, **yet** I'm nervous about it too. (**Yet** presents a contrast.)

3. Transitions are words and phrases such as *however, therefore, in addition, consequently, in fact, first, second,* and *finally*. We use them to connect ideas between sentences or larger expanses of text.

   Cars cause pollution. **In addition,** they create traffic jams. (**In addition** adds information.)
   Cars are too prominent in our society to be gotten rid of. **Nevertheless,** we will have to do something to address the problems they create. (**Nevertheless** presents a contrast.)

4. Be careful! Some people object to beginning a written sentence with a coordinating conjunction, particularly in academic writing. However, some writers use coordinating conjunctions to connect ideas from sentence to sentence.

   connects ideas within sentence
   I hate driving, **so** I took the bus.
   connects ideas from one sentence to another
   I hate driving. **So** I took the bus.

5. Punctuation of compound sentences: When coordinating conjunctions are used to join two independent clauses in a compound sentence, these conjunctions are generally preceded by a comma.

   Cars are beneficial, **but** they cause many problems.

6. Placement of coordinating conjunctions: Coordinating conjunctions are placed only at the beginning of a clause, not within it or at the end of it.

   I was hungry, **so** I made a sandwich.
   OR
   I was hungry. **So** I made a sandwich.
   NOT ~~I was hungry, I so made a sandwich.~~
   OR
   ~~I was hungry, I made a sandwich, so.~~

7. Placement of transitions: Transitions can come at the beginning of a sentence, within it, or at the end, depending on what the writer or speaker wants to emphasize. They are usually separated from the rest of the sentence by a comma or commas.

   However, cars are harmful as well as beneficial.
   Cars, **however,** are harmful as well as beneficial.
   Cars are harmful as well as beneficial, **however.**

(continued on next page)

8. Types of transitions:

a. The following transitions add information: *also, in addition (to), additionally, for one thing, moreover, furthermore, plus, besides (that), for example, for instance, likewise, in fact, along with, indeed.*

Cars have caused people to forsake public transportation. **Moreover,** they've led to the construction of gigantic shopping malls.

b. The following transitions offer contrasting information to an idea presented earlier: *however, still, nevertheless, in contrast, in fact, instead, in spite of (this), despite (this), on the contrary, on the other hand.*

Cars cause many problems. **However,** it would be difficult to live without them.

c. The following transitions present a cause for or a result of an action or situation discussed earlier: *therefore, thus, because (of this), on account of (this), consequently, accordingly, otherwise, as a result.*

Cars make it possible to live far away from the workplace. **Thus,** more animal and plant habitats are destroyed each year to make way for new homes.

d. The following transitions show the relation of actions, events, or ideas in time: *next, then, afterwards, meanwhile, after that, first, second, third, finally, in conclusion, to sum up.*

I had a series of disasters. **First,** the car broke down. **Next,** it was impounded by a policeman.

These transitions are also commonly used to show the organization and presentation of a writer's or speaker's ideas.

First, cars have vastly increased our mobility. **Second,** cars have given people more freedom. **Finally,** the car industry provides employment.

Note: Some transitions can function in more than one category. See Grammar Note 11.

See Appendix 22 on page A25 for a more complete list of transitions.

9. Punctuation of transitions: Be careful! Be sure to place a period or a semicolon—not a comma—before a transition when it is the first word in a sentence or clause. A comma in this location is incorrect and creates an error called a comma splice.

She has a car. **However,** she rarely uses it.

OR

She has a car; **however,** she rarely uses it.

NOT ~~She has a car, **however,** she rarely uses it.~~

See From Grammar to Writing after Part VIII, page 302, for further discussion of comma splices.

10. Be careful! Do not confuse subordinating conjunctions with transitions.

The train is old and dirty. **However,** it gets me to work. NOT ~~The train is old and dirty. **Although** it gets me to work.~~

11. *Though* can be a subordinating conjunction or a transition.

subordinating conjunction

Though cars have become increasingly expensive, nearly everyone finds a way to afford them.

transition meaning *however*

Jobs, **though,** aren't everything.

In fact can both add and contrast.

I'm very fond of train rides. **In fact,** trains are the most civilized way to travel. (adds)

Many people believe that planes are unsafe. **In fact,** they're statistically safer than cars. (contrasts)

The coordinating conjunction *or (else)* can have two meanings.

You can take the metro, **or (else)** you can go by bus. (adds an alternative)

Make your payment, **or (else)** we'll repossess your car. (suggests a consequence)

FOCUSED PRACTICE

1. Discover the Grammar

Read the newspaper article and underline transitions and coordinating conjunctions if they join independent clauses or sentences. Above each, write what the transition or coordinating conjunction presents: an addition, a contrast, a result, a cause, or a relation in time. You will find seven coordinating conjunctions and sixteen transitions.

The Concord Clarion

Take the Train? Well, Maybe . . .

by John Baca

Readers of our newspaper know that we favor the increased use and development of mass transit over the building of more highways. For years we've supported those who have been calling for the development of a regional transportation network whose components would be heavy rail, using existing tracks that the big trains run on; light rail, which would mean building new tracks that trolleys and small trains could run on; better bus service; and a metro system. Heavy rail tracks are already there, so (result) heavy rail has gotten the most favorable press.

It occurred to our chief editor, however, that maybe someone should be sent to find out whether trains are really as efficient and pleasant as they're cracked up to be. I've written a lot of articles on transportation in the last several years, so I was the logical choice to do the investigation because I was considered an "expert." Therefore, I confidently set out on my journey one rainy Saturday morning.

I took the bus downtown to the train station, bought a ticket for Santa Maria, just 100 miles away, and went out on the platform to wait for the 9:02. That's when the train trip from hell began. Everything that could go wrong did go wrong.

First, the train was an hour late. Also, we were at the height of the tourist season, so when it finally did arrive, there seemed to be at least a million people waiting to board it. The quick rushed on, mercilessly elbowing the slow out of their way. I finally managed to board and tried to find a seat. There wasn't one, though; I had to stand with five other people in the space between two cars. I was right next to the men's restroom, which did not exactly smell like a flower garden. In fact, to say that it smelled like a garbage dump would have been too charitable.

For half an hour or so the train just sat on the track, not moving. A man standing next to me with extremely bad breath insisted on telling me his life story. I listened politely for a while; then I excused myself, saying that I hadn't eaten breakfast. Meanwhile, the train had started, so I swayed back and forth on my way to the dining car, propelled violently by the motion of the now-moving cars.

As I was entering the dining car, a violent lurch of the train threw me to the left, causing me to lose my balance and land in the lap of a portly woman drinking coffee, which spilled on both of us. I apologized profusely. My apology, however, was apparently not convincing, for the woman just glared at me. I got up and went to order tea and a sandwich, which cost me $8.95, from an impolite attendant. The tea was lukewarm and virtually flavorless, and the sandwich tasted like a combination of sawdust and cardboard. I wended my way back to my starting place, but there still wasn't a vacant seat. I was forced to spend the next hour and a half listening to the same man tell his life history all over again.

By the time the train finally arrived in Santa Maria, two hours late, I had come to several conclusions as to why more people don't take the train, if ours was any indication. First, trains are extremely slow; it had taken four hours to go 100 miles. Second, the train was filthy and uninviting. Third, train personnel were generally surly and unhelpful. Fourth, the tracks were in terrible condition.

So does this all mean that I'm now anti-train and pro-highway? No, I'm still a supporter of mass transit. However, I've learned that the situation isn't nearly as simple as we at the newspaper have been portraying it. All over the country we've allowed trains to deteriorate. We must make them viable again if we expect people to use them. We've got to demand excellent, efficient service. That will take money, perhaps (gasp!) even a tax increase. Nonetheless, it would be well worth it.

2. Disaster

Listen to the following segment of a radio newscast. It was recorded during a thunderstorm, and static makes it impossible to hear some parts of it. Listen again while you read the text. Think about what needs to go into each blank and write in the appropriate connector. Choose words and phrases from the box.

meanwhile	otherwise	first	in fact
however	therefore	and	second
also	next		

____Next____ (1.) we focus on the aftermath of the recent California earthquake.

Investigators have determined that it will cost billions of dollars to rebuild damaged highways. According to the governor, two actions have to be taken: ________ (2.), the federal government will have to approve disaster funds to pay for reconstruction; ________ (3.), insurance investigators will have to determine how much their companies will have to pay in the rebuilding effort. With luck, the governor says, some key highways could be rebuilt within six months.

He cautioned, ________ (4.), that the six-month figure is only an estimate; the process depends on timely allocation of funds, and certain insurance companies have in the past been notoriously slow to approve such funds. The rebuilding effort could, ________ (5.), drag on for at least a year. ________ (6.), bad weather could hamper the speedy completion of the project.

________ (7.), it is taking some people as long as four hours to commute to work, and others haven't been able to get to work at all. Interviewed by our news team, one commuter who works in an office downtown, some forty miles from her home, said, "This has been ridiculous. It took me six hours to drive to work last Friday. I knew I'd have to find some other way of getting there; ________ (8.), I'd never make it. Well, yesterday I took the train and arrived there in fifty minutes. ________ (9.) you know, the trip was really pleasant. I got the chance to read the morning paper. ________ (10.), I think I'm going to switch permanently to the train."

3. Public Transportation

A public panel has met and made recommendations for improving the local transportation system. Complete their recommendations by choosing one of the two transitions in parentheses to connect each pair of sentences.

1. Widespread use of public transportation is better for the environment than reliance on the automobile. It will be cheaper in the long run, _____also_____ (though / also). We need to de-emphasize the use of cars.
2. We must develop better mass-transit systems. __________ (However / Thus), we must also find a way to pay for them. An increased sales tax may be the best source of revenue.
3. Many cities around the world are building underground metro systems, but these will take time to construct. __________ (Moreover / Meanwhile), citizens will have to depend on bus transport. We need to expand bus service.
4. Mass transit systems must be made attractive and convenient; __________ (otherwise / on the contrary), people will not use them. Our regional system must be pleasing to the patrons.
5. Some people are afraid to fly because they believe they have a better chance to survive a car accident than a plane crash. __________ (In fact / Likewise), airplanes are much safer statistically than automobiles. Our task force supports expanded air travel and the building of a new airport.
6. In many European cities, the transportation systems make it pleasant, easy, and relatively cheap to get around fast. In Paris, __________ (on the other hand / for example), you can buy a metro pass that is good for three days on an underground system that goes nearly everywhere. That's the sort of incentive plan we need in our new system.
7. The cost of digging a subway has increased geometrically in the last twenty years. __________ (Because of this / Afterwards), it will cost far more, proportionately, for cities without subway systems to build them than it would have cost had they been built before 1970. We need to de-emphasize subway construction and push for light rail.
8. We will have great difficulty persuading people to use mass transit instead of their cars, for most individuals will make strong arguments in favor of continuing to go everywhere by car. __________ (Nonetheless / Accordingly), there are compelling reasons for trying to persuade them. Our group feels that we can persuade the public if we mount the right sort of campaign.

4. Editing

Find and correct the twelve mistakes in the use of discourse connectors, providing a correct connector in each case. You may add or delete words, but do not change word order or punctuation.

MY CAR IS MOVING TO THE SUBURBS

by James Marx

The other day I was driving on the Evergreen Expressway, ~~also~~ *and* a policeman stopped me for speeding. I had to pay a ninety-dollar fine, in spite of I was going only seven miles per hour over the speed limit. That was the last straw. I've decided that I'm going to send my car to a new home in the suburbs.

I used to think that a car was the most wonderful thing in the world. I loved the freedom of being able to come and go to my part-time job or to the college whenever I wanted. A year ago I was in a car pool with four other people, however I hated having to wait on account of my car pool members weren't ready to leave.

Although, I've changed my mind since then. Now it's clear to me that there are just too many disadvantages to having a car in town. For one thing, sitting stalled in your car in a traffic jam is stressful, besides it's a phenomenal waste of time. In addition, it costs me $200 a month to park my car in the city, also there's always the chance it will be vandalized.

Because, I've decided to leave it at my cousin Brent's house in the suburbs. Or, I'll end up going broke paying parking costs. My car will have a good home, also I'll use it just for longer trips. When I'm in the city, although, I'll take the bus or the trolley, otherwise I'll walk. Who knows? They say that you can meet some interesting people on the bus. Maybe I'll find the love of my life.

COMMUNICATION PRACTICE

5. Practice Listening

Alice Wu is a driver's license examiner. Listen to her statements to people about how they did on their exams. Then circle the letter of the sentence that correctly restates her meaning.

1. (a.) Though Mr. Matos could use some practice in parallel parking, he passed the exam.
   b. Because Mr. Matos could use some practice in parallel parking, he passed the exam.
2. a. Mrs. Adams failed the exam because, in addition to handling the car well, she ran a red light.
   b. Mrs. Adams failed the exam because, despite handling the car well, she ran a red light.
3. a. If Bob had turned his wheels away from the curb, he would have passed.
   b. If Bob had turned his wheels away from the curb, he still wouldn't have passed.
4. a. Jan signaled neither to turn left nor to stop.
   b. Jan signaled to stop but not to turn left.
5. a. Dr. Thomas passed the exam, for he scraped the curb.
   b. Dr. Thomas passed the exam, but he scraped the curb when he parked.
6. a. Because Deborah failed the written exam, she can't take the road test yet.
   b. Because Deborah can't take the road test yet, she failed the written exam.
7. a. Ms. Hanai needs to work both on hand signals and parking.
   b. Ms. Hanai needs to work on hand signals but not parking.
8. a. Ambrose's California license expired before he took the written exam.
   b. Ambrose's California license expired after he took the written exam.

6. Tape Discussion

Are driver's license requirements strict enough?

7. Small Group Discussion

Divide into small groups. Begin with the statements here and make additional statements, using the transitions given. Write your sentences down and then report them to the class later.

1. Cars give us mobility. (*also, furthermore, however, besides that*)

   Example:

   A: Also, they give us freedom.
   B: Furthermore, it's difficult to do without a car.
   C: However, they are getting very expensive.
   D: Besides that, it's hard to find a place to park.

2. Car insurance is quite expensive. (*in addition, moreover, because of this, nevertheless*)
3. Trains are an efficient means of transportation. (*for one thing, therefore, though, plus the fact that*)
4. Flying is a good way to travel. (*for example, in fact, however, consequently*)

8. Role Play in Groups

Work in small groups and role-play one of the following situations. Then reverse the roles and play the situation again.

1. A bystander has witnessed a hit-and-run accident and is talking to a police officer who is investigating the situation.

   Example:

   Officer: OK, ma'am, can you tell me what you saw?
   Bystander: Yeah. I was just starting to cross the intersection when I saw the little girl who was hit start to cross from the other side. We had the walk signal. A red Honda Accord was coming really fast from the opposite direction. It slowed down just before the intersection. **However,** it didn't stop. The driver hit the girl and went on through the intersection. . . .

2. A teenager wants permission to buy a car. The parents can't afford to buy another car, but the teenager is willing to work to pay for it. They are discussing the situation.
3. A married couple are planning a vacation. One spouse wants to drive, and the other wants to go by train. They are trying to come to some agreement.
4. A couple have just gone to a movie. Coming out of the movie theater, they have discovered that their car has been towed. They are convinced that the car was towed illegally and are talking to the head of the towing company.

9. Essay

Choose one of the following topics and write an essay of three or four paragraphs on it.

Topic 1. One way to reduce or eliminate automobile pollution is . . .
Topic 2. To persuade people to use their cars responsibly, we need to . . .
Topic 3. Mass transit isn't necessarily the answer to our transportation problems.

10. Picture Discussion

This painting shows a scene from America's past. The road in the picture was considered a highway. How has transportation changed since that time? As a class, discuss how transportation has changed in other countries around the world.

Example:

In ________________, most people ride bicycles. **However,** more and more people are buying cars.

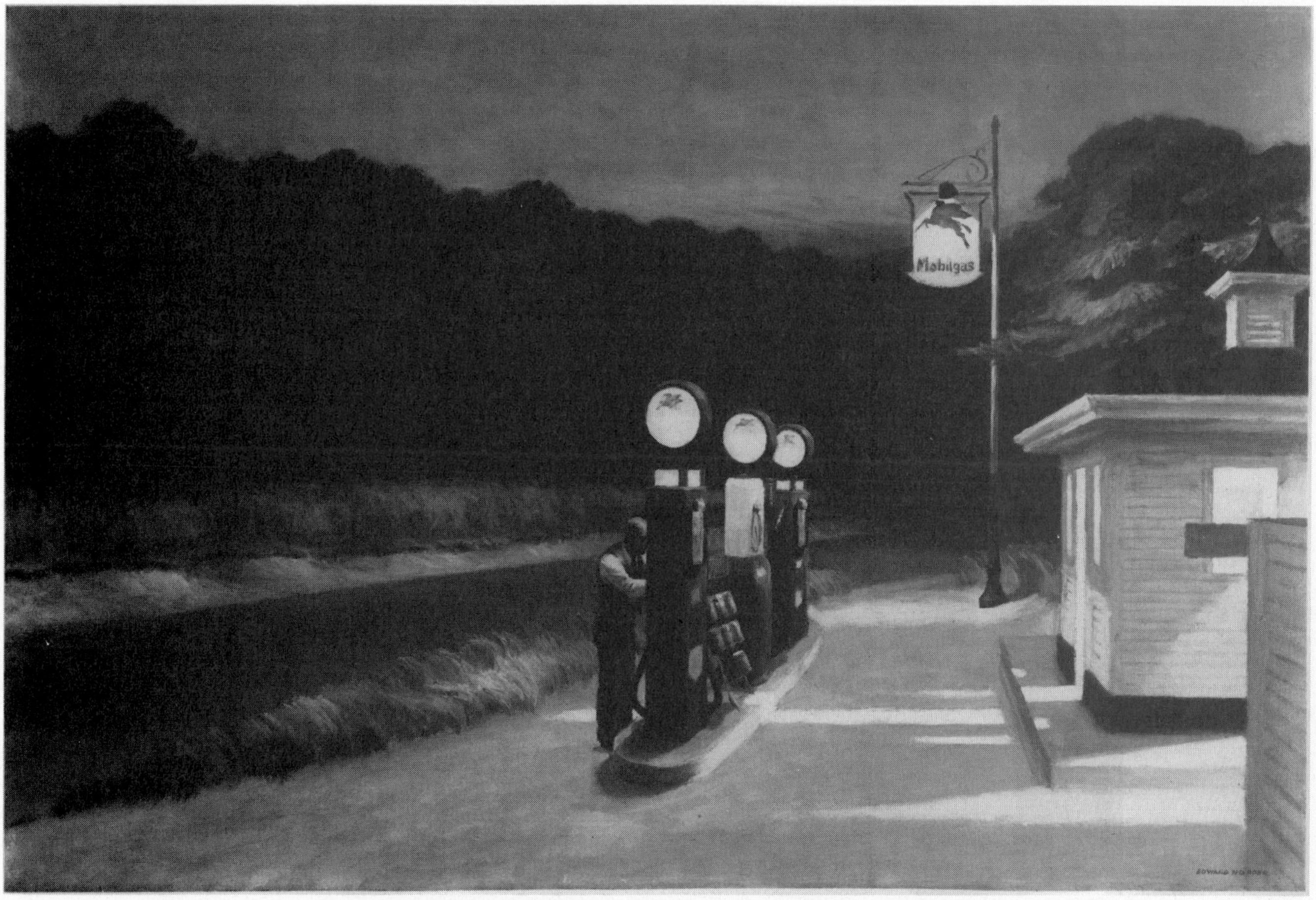

Edward Hopper: *Gas.* (1940) Oil on canvas, 26 1/4 x 40 1/4".
The Museum of Modern Art, New York. Mrs. Simon Guggenheim Fund.
Photograph ©1995 The Museum of Modern Art, New York.

UNIT 15

Adverbial Modifying Phrases

INTRODUCTION

Read and listen to the script of a student's speech to a class.

Questions to Consider

1. What are some serious problems facing the world today?
2. Do you think overpopulation is one of them?

Millions and Millions

Today the population of Planet Earth is more than five-and-a-half billion, an increase of one-and-a-half billion in only eighteen years. There are more of us every minute, and the more people there are, of course, the greater the strain on the world's resources. By the year 2020, the world's population is expected to exceed eight billion. **Observing that population always increases geometrically while the food supply increases arithmetically,** nineteenth-century economist Thomas Malthus gave us an early warning of the problem we now face. There will never be any more water on the earth's surface than there is now, but there will be more people. **By using new methods of farming and newly developed, higher-yield crops,** farmers have been able to increase the amount of available food, but this can't go on forever. Can they continuously expand the food supply to match the population growth? It doesn't seem likely.

How did we arrive at this situation? There are two principal forces operating: a vast increase in the number of people, caused in part by advances in medicine and health; and the revolution of rising expectations. **Having wiped out smallpox,** scientists now contemplate the elimination of polio and other diseases. Infant mortality rates, while still tragically high in many nations, have been declining worldwide. People are living much longer than they used to; in many nations the life expectancy is seventy-five years and rising.

Meanwhile, the increasing trend toward a world economy has made more and more products available to more and more people, **straining the world's resources.** It is reasonable, a natural consequence of a rising standard of living, for people to want what others have. Eventually, however, this desire will have to be controlled. The population will continue to increase, but the amount and number of natural resources won't.

What can we do to solve the problem? Should we (1) colonize other planets? (2) Let "nature take its course" **by allowing wars to reduce the number of people?** (3) Create a world government which controls the world food supply and forcibly limits the number of children a couple can have? These measures seem draconian or fanciful; isn't there a more realistic or humane solution? Some say that, **to prevent a future disaster,** we must achieve Zero Population Growth, or ZPG, everywhere on the planet. How would it work? **Having reached childbearing age,** parents would limit themselves to no more than two children—the replacement level. This procedure would supposedly cause population to eventually stabilize and later decline. But could this really happen? And wouldn't it violate the sincere beliefs, legitimate rights, and religious liberty of many people?

A real-life example illustrates the situation. **Faced with an increasingly large population,** now nearing 1.2 billion, the government of China has for some time had a policy of permitting only one child per family. The effect has been a slower rate of population growth than in the past.

However, the Chinese solution may not be every country's solution. **If presented with proposals to adopt the Chinese program in their own nations,** in fact, many people might object violently, **considering such measures harsh, immoral, and out of the question.** It seems clear, though, that **to prevent major war, outbreaks of disease, and increased poverty,** all nations will eventually have to address the problem of population growth, which I consider our most serious worldwide dilemma today.

ADVERBIAL MODIFYING PHRASES

WITH A PRESENT PARTICIPLE
Recognizing that hunger is a problem, we must take steps to eliminate it.
Not wanting to commit himself, the president declined to be specific.

WITH *BY* + PRESENT PARTICIPLE
By using new agricultural methods and higher-yield crops, farmers have been able to increase the amount of food.

WITH A PAST PARTICIPLE
Given two options, we will choose the one that results in the greatest good for the greatest number.
When asked if he would support the treaty, the president wouldn't give a clear answer.

WITH *HAVING* + PAST PARTICIPLE
Having conquered many deadly diseases, scientists are now trying to develop a vaccine for AIDS.

PHRASES REDUCED FROM CLAUSES
While talking with an expert on homelessness, I learned a great deal.

Grammar Notes

1. In Unit 12, we studied sentences made up of independent clauses and dependent adverbial clauses. We saw how clauses enable speakers and writers to combine thoughts in such a way that precise connections between the ideas become clear.

   adverbial clause
   Because the population of the country had increased dramatically, there was a severe shortage of adequate housing.

   Similarly, we can link ideas clearly by using modifying phrases which modify the ideas and actions in independent clauses.

   adverbial modifying phrase
   Having conquered many deadly diseases, scientists are trying to develop a vaccine for AIDS.

   In this sentence, the adverbial modifying phrase, "having conquered many deadly diseases," modifies the main (or independent) clause, "scientists are trying to develop a vaccine for AIDS." The sentence above can be seen as a combination of the following two underlying ideas:

   Scientists have conquered many deadly diseases. They are trying to develop a vaccine for AIDS.

   Remember that a clause contains a subject and a verb. A phrase does not.

2. Two sentences can be combined into one sentence with an independent clause and an adverbial modifying phrase if their subjects refer to the same person, place, or thing. In sentences of this type, the adverbial modifying phrase can come either before or after the main clause, though it more commonly appears first.

   modifying phrase
   By taking significant measures now,
   independent clause
   we can prevent overpopulation.

   independent clause
   We can prevent overpopulation
   modifying phrase
   by taking significant measures now.

3. There are five main types of adverbial phrases.

   a. With a present participle: Use this form when you are talking about two actions or events that occurred in the same general time frame. Place the idea that you consider more important in the independent clause. Then replace the subject and verb from the subordinate idea with a present participle.

   Nineteenth-century economist Thomas Malthus observed that population always increases geometrically while the food supply increases arithmetically.

   PLUS

   He gave us an early warning of the problem we now face.

   BECOMES

   Observing that population always increases geometrically while the food supply increases arithmetically, nineteenth-century economist Thomas Malthus gave us an early warning of the problem we now face.

   OR

   Nineteenth-century economist Thomas Malthus gave us an early warning of the problem we now face, **observing that population always increases geometrically while the food supply increases arithmetically.** (Both original actions, **observing** and **giving**, occurred in the same general time frame.)

   The prime minister didn't want to publicize the details of the treaty. PLUS The prime minister refused to speak to the press. = **Not wanting to publicize the details of the treaty,** the prime minister refused to speak to the press.

(continued on next page)

b. With *by* plus a present participle: Use this form when there is a clear sense of intention or purpose—i.e., that one action causes a certain result. Replace the subject and verb with *by* plus a present participle.

The Chinese government encouraged single-child families.

PLUS

The Chinese government attacked the problem of overpopulation.

BECOMES

By encouraging single-child families, the Chinese government attacked the problem of overpopulation.

OR

The Chinese government attacked the problem of overpopulation **by encouraging single-child families.** (The Chinese government used this means to attack the problem.)

c. With a past participle: Use this form when you want to communicate a passive meaning. Replace a subject and auxiliary with a past participle.

People are presented with proposals to adopt the Chinese program in their own nations.

PLUS

Many people might object violently.

BECOMES

Presented with proposals to adopt the Chinese program in their own nations, many people might object violently.

OR

Many people might object violently, **presented with proposals to adopt the Chinese program in their own nations.** (The writer wants to include a passive idea—that people will be presented with certain proposals—in order to focus on their objections.)

d. With *having* plus a past participle: Use this form when you are talking about actions or events that occurred at different times. Replace the subject and verb with *having* + past participle.

past

Scientists **wiped out** smallpox.

PLUS

present

They now **contemplate** the elimination of polio and other diseases.

BECOMES

Scientists now contemplate the elimination of polio and other diseases, **having wiped out smallpox.**

OR

Having wiped out smallpox, scientists now contemplate the elimination of polio and other diseases. (The wiping out of smallpox occurred earlier in time.)

e. Reduced from adverb clauses: Some adverbial phrases are actually a reduced form of an adverbial clause that contained *be* and a subordinating word such as *although, even though, if, though, unless, until, when, whenever, while.* To reduce a clause in this way, delete the subject and auxiliary verb from the adverbial clause.

If they are carried out right, proposals to reduce the population might work.

BECOMES

If carried out right, proposals to reduce the population might work.

When he was asked if he would support the treaty, the president wouldn't give a clear answer.

BECOMES

When asked if he would support the treaty, the president wouldn't give a clear answer.

While I was talking with an expert on homelessness, I learned a great deal.

BECOMES

While talking with an expert on homelessness, I learned a great deal.

Note that in the examples above, the phrase can be further reduced by eliminating the subordinating word as well.

If carried out right, proposals to reduce the population might work.

BECOMES

Carried out right, proposals to reduce the population might work.

4. The infinitive of purpose is often used adverbially. Use this form when there is an infinitive phrase and a sense of purpose involved in the action. Delete the subject and verb.

We want to prevent war, disease, and poverty.

PLUS

We must do something major and comprehensive.

BECOMES

To prevent war, disease, and poverty, we must do something major and comprehensive.

OR

We must do something major and comprehensive **to prevent war, disease, and poverty.** (Note existence of infinitive phrase and clear sense of purpose.)

The sentence with the adverbial phrase can also be written with *in order to.*

In order to prevent war, disease, and poverty, we must do something major and comprehensive.

5. Be careful! If we combine (with an adverbial phrase) two sentences whose subjects are different, we create an incorrect, illogical sentence. This error is called a dangling modifier because the phrase we create "dangles," having nothing in the sentence to modify. The following two sentences cannot be combined.

subject

The **population** of China had increased tremendously.

PLUS

subject

Government **officials** had to take significant measures.

CANNOT BE COMBINED AS

~~Having increased tremendously in population, Chinese government officials had to take significant measures~~.

The phrase with *having* is a dangling modifier. It has nothing in the sentence to modify. The government officials did not increase in population, so the sentence is incorrect and illogical. The problem arises from joining two sentences whose subjects are different: *population* and *officials*.

To make sure that two sentences have the same subjects, draw a rectangle around each subject and connect the two rectangles with an arrow. If they refer to the same person or thing, they can be combined logically and correctly.

[Farmers] are using new methods. [They] can increase the amount of available food.

The two subjects, *farmers* and *they*, refer to the same thing, so the combination is clear and logical.

(By) using new methods, farmers can increase the amount of available food.

FOCUSED PRACTICE

1. Discover the Grammar

Listen to the following newscast on the tape. Then look at the text of the newscast and underline all of the adverbial phrases.

Good afternoon. This is news to the hour from the World Broadcasting Network.

☐ The cease-fire has been broken in Franconia. When asked whether he would attend the upcoming peace conference in Geneva, dissident leader Amalde declined to commit himself, saying that the success of the conference depends on the good-faith actions of Mr. Tintor, the country's president. Mr. Amalde went on to say that Mr. Tintor could demonstrate good faith by agreeing to free and unconditional talks. Interviewed about Mr. Amalde's comments, an aide to President Tintor, speaking on condition of anonymity, said that he did not expect the peace conference to take place as planned.

☐ Meanwhile, researchers from the Global Health Foundation announced plans to test a new vaccine for AIDS. Acknowledging that the current vaccine is ineffective, the researchers claim that their new vaccine is a marked improvement over the old one and believe that it holds great promise.

☐ Scientists at WASA, the World Aeronautics and Space Association, announced plans to launch a new space telescope with four times the magnification power of the existing space instrument. Having conducted successful repairs and identified flaws on Magna Maria, WASA's existing instrument, the agency is confident that the new telescope will be well worth its billion-dollar price tag.

☐ Finally, a new nation comes into existence at midnight tonight. To be known as Illyria, the new nation has been carved out of the eastern portion of Spartania. According to its new president, Illyria will need massive infusions of foreign aid to be a viable state.

☐ That's news to the hour; stay tuned for breaking developments.

2. World Concerns

Draw a rectangle around the subject in each pair of sentences. Connect the pairs of rectangles with an arrow. Then say whether the two sentences can be correctly combined or not.

1. Scientists have eliminated smallpox. They are trying to find a vaccine for AIDS. (yes) no
2. The standard of living has risen worldwide. New problems have been created. yes no
3. The population increases geometrically. The food supply increases arithmetically. yes no
4. Governments seek to prevent unrest. They must ensure the welfare of the majority. yes no
5. Many parents want more than two children. These people oppose ZPG. yes no
6. Governmental leaders feel that they propose workable solutions. Citizens often disagree. yes no

3. The Problem of Poverty

Writer Jim Lamoreaux has just returned from an assignment in Latin America. He is preparing a talk about his trip to a group of citizens. Shorten his sentences by reducing each adverbial clause to an adverbial phrase. Place the subject in the independent clause, and eliminate the subject and form of the verb **be** *from the dependent clause.*

1. While tourists from wealthy nations are enjoying their vacations in poor nations, they don't realize how desperate the lives of people they see on the streets may be.

   While enjoying their vacations in poor nations, tourists from wealthy nations don't realize how desperate the lives of people they see on the street may be.

2. When some tourists are giving money to beggars on the street, they mistakenly think they are doing their part to help the poor.

   ____

3. Tourists cannot truly understand the plight of the poor unless they are provided with firsthand knowledge of poverty.

   ____

4. If orphans in poor countries are sponsored by people in wealthier nations, they can escape the cycle of poverty.

   ____

5. Poor people will not be able to escape poverty until they are given job opportunities.

   ____

4. Human Interest

Jim Lamoreaux has sold an article on his trip to Outlook *magazine. Read and carefully study the article. It contains eleven sentences with adverbial modifying phrases. Five are correct; six are wrong because they contain dangling modifiers. Underline all of the incorrect sentences.*

A Helping Hand

BY JIM LAMOREAUX

If you are at all like me, you tire of requests to help others. Barraged by seemingly constant appeals for money to support public television, the Policemen's Benevolent Association, or the Special Olympics, worthy organizations all, I tend to tune out, my brain numbed. It's not that I'm selfish, I don't think; it's just that there are so many of these requests. Subjected to many stimuli, only the crucial ones stick in my mind. By arguing that I don't have enough money anyway, the request is ignored. At least that was the way I saw the situation until the magazine I write for sent me to a small village overseas to do a human-interest story on homeless children.

Having seen and heard numerous television requests to sponsor a child overseas, I had always said to myself, "I'll bet the money gets pocketed by some local politician." My opinion changed after I got to know Elena and after I saw the reality of her life.

Having landed in the capital city, a taxi took me to my hotel in the center of town, and that's where I met her. Sitting on a dirty blanket on the sidewalk in front of the hotel, my eye was caught by her. She didn't beg; instead she was trying to scratch out a semblance of a living by selling matches. Smiling up at me, she asked, with almost no accent, "Matches, sir?" I bought some matches, and we got to talking. Her parents were both dead, and she lived with an elderly English-speaking great-aunt who had no job but sold firewood for money. I eventually learned from the great-aunt that Elena had suffered from polio at the age of five and now walked with a distinct limp.

While talking later with a nun at a nearby covent that administers gift money from other countries, much worthwhile information was given to me. She proved to my satisfaction that money from sponsors does indeed get to those who need it. Finding that I could sponsor Elena for fifty cents a day, I began to be ashamed; I spend more than that on my dogs. But what remains most vivid in my mind is my vision of Elena. She didn't beg, and she didn't feel sorry for herself. Selling her matches, her spirit shone through, simply trying to scratch out a semblance of a living. So I say to you reading this: The next time you hear an ad about sponsoring a child, pay attention.

5. World Issues

Combine each of the following pairs of sentences into one sentence with an independent clause and an adverbial phrase, using the form in parentheses.

1. We want to make the world safer. We must outlaw chemical and biological warfare. (infinitive)

   To make the world safer, we must outlaw chemical and biological warfare.

2. We are given the choice between disaster and some kind of restriction on our right to have as many children as we want. We may have to choose the latter. (past participle)

3. The world's population grew slowly between the years 500 and 1700. It then began to accelerate. (*having* + past participle)

4. Farmers all over the world clear more and more land for farms every year. They unfortunately destroy animal habitats. (present participle)

5. Many governments want to ensure that their citizens are healthy. They provide immunizations to all children. (infinitive)

6. Health officials in some countries provide contraceptive devices to their citizens. They are trying to deal with the problem of overpopulation. (*by* + present participle)

7. We must stabilize the world's population growth. We need to prevent ecological disaster. (infinitive)

8. We have witnessed two devastating conflicts in this century. We must do everything in our power to prevent future world wars. (*having* + past participle)

6. Editing

Each of the following sentences from a student's exam in a World Problems class contains an incorrect adverbial phrase. Correct each sentence.

1. Giving the options of doing nothing or of controlling population growth, we must choose the latter.

   Given the options of doing nothing or of controlling population growth, we must choose the latter.

2. To observe that population and food supply grow at different rates, Malthus warned us of a problem.

3. Preventing unrest, governments everywhere must ensure full employment.

4. Recognized that overpopulation was a problem, the Chinese government took action.

5. Established a policy of limiting births, Chinese government officials now have to enforce it.

6. Leaders of governments throughout the world must do something comprehensive having prevented a major disaster.

7. If carrying out right, the adoption of ZPG would cause the population to decrease.

8. By we sponsor a needy child in the Third World, we make the world a little better.

COMMUNICATION PRACTICE

7. Practice Listening

UNESCO expert Galina Malchevskaya is giving a talk to a class of college students. Listen to their conversation on the tape. Then listen again and circle the letter of the sentence that explains the meaning of certain of Ms. Malchevskaya's sentences.

1. a. Scientists will wipe out smallpox soon.
   (b.) Scientists wiped out smallpox.
2. a. A cure for AIDS has been discovered.
   b. A cure for AIDS hasn't been discovered.
3. a. We can prevent disaster if we ignore the need for population control.
   b. We can't prevent disaster if we ignore the need for population control.
4. a. Zero Population Growth has already been achieved.
   b. Zero Population Growth has not yet been achieved.
5. a. With ZPG, couples would not have more than two children.
   b. With ZPG, couples would reach childbearing age having had two children.
6. a. ZPG could work if it were carried out properly.
   b. If ZPG reduced the number of people properly, it would be carried out.
7. a. Someone would present proposals to us.
   b. We would present proposals to someone.
8. a. We have already arrived at a comprehensive solution for each country.
   b. We haven't yet arrived at a comprehensive solution for each country.
9. a. War and poverty have been prevented.
   b. War and poverty have not been prevented.
10. a. Higher-yield crops will be developed in the future.
    b. Higher-yield crops have already been developed.

8. Pair and Group Discussion

With a partner, write sentences expressing your opinions for or against the statements about the following topics. Then share your opinions with the class.

Topic 1. We need to solve the problem of overpopulation.

Example: We *do* need to solve the problem of overpopulation. **To solve the problem of overpopulation,** we need to think about limiting births.

Topic 2. We need to persuade people to accept ZPG.
Topic 3. We can improve the lot of homeless people.

9. Debate

It is the year 2025. A colony on the asteroid Ceres has run out of space and resources. A law is being proposed making it illegal for a couple to have more than two children. Divide into two groups: those supporting the law and those opposing it. Within your group, prepare your argument. Then have a debate on the issue.

10. Essay

Choose one of the following topics and write a short essay of three or four paragraphs about it. Try to use at least four of the five types of adverbial phrases in your essay.

Topic 1. Having carefully thought about the problem of overpopulation, I believe . . .
Topic 2. To persuade people that overpopulation is an extremely serious problem, . . .
Topic 3. Given the choice between letting events follow their current course and making some serious changes, . . .

11. Picture Discussion

The addition of bovine growth hormone to cattle feed is one method of increasing milk production. Its use has caused considerable controversy. With a partner, prepare the script of an impartial news report about the recent availability of this product in your community.

I. *Read the conversations. Underline all adverb clauses.*

1. **A:** Honey, we're going to be late <u>if we don't leave right now</u>.
   B: OK. We can leave as soon as you back the car out of the garage.
2. **A:** Harry is a lot more responsible than he used to be.
   B: Yeah, I know. He never used to do his chores unless I threatened him. Now he does things.
3. **A:** I'll call you when the plane gets in.
   B: OK, but you'd better take down Ida's number in case I'm not home.
4. **A:** Wasn't that a great dinner? I ate so much that I can hardly move.
   B: Yeah. Dad is such a fabulous cook that I end up gaining a few pounds whenever I come home to visit.
5. **A:** You know, there aren't as many good shows as there used to be.
   B: Oh, I don't know. You have access to some pretty impressive programming—provided that you have cable.
6. **A:** Joe, since you didn't turn in your term paper, you didn't pass the course—even though you did well on the tests.
   B: Yes, I know. I didn't do it because I couldn't think of anything to write about.

II. *Choose transitions from the box to complete the news item. Use each transition only once.*

otherwise	however	thus
moreover	in fact	next

We focus ___next___ (1.) on the mission of the Ares, the manned space mission of WASA, the World Aeronautics and Space Association. The Ares was launched seven months ago from Woomera Spaceport in Australia. ________ (2.), contact had been lost with the Ares for the past three weeks, and WASA officials had feared the worst. WASA officials were ________ (3.) elated when they received a radio message today that the Ares has made a successful landing on Mars. Harald Svendorf, chief of WASA, had this to say in today's news conference: "We needed a victory; ________ (4.), we might have lost our United Nations funding. This successful landing should silence our critics, who have been calling the Ares Project a boondoggle. The project will ________ (5.) be one of the most cost-effective missions in the history of space exploration. ________ (6.), it will pave the way toward realization of other manned missions to the Jovian moons and to Venus."

III. *Combine the two sentences into one sentence with a dependent clause and an independent clause. Use the indicated subordinating conjunction.*

1. Mel and Sarah Figueroa were in a difficult situation. They both had jobs and didn't have day care for their two children. (because)

   Mel and Sarah Figueroa were in a difficult situation because they both had jobs and didn't have day care for their two children.

2. They had been leaving the children with Sarah's mother. This wasn't a satisfactory situation. (though)

3. One of them was going to have to quit working. They could find a solution to the problem. (unless)

4. One of their neighbors proposed the creation of a day care co-op involving seven families. Their problem was solved. (when)

5. Each day, one of the parents in the co-op cares for all of the children. The other parents are working. (while)

IV. *Correct the eight mistakes in negative and focus adverbs in the letter.*

Dear Samantha,

I wanted to thank you again for your hospitality while we were in Vancouver. Not only ^did you and Michael ~~showed~~ show us a wonderful time, but we got to re-establish the close ties we used to have. The even kids enjoyed the trip, and you know how kids can be on vacations. Only I hope that Dan and I can reciprocate sometime.

The drive back to Edmonton was something else; almost we didn't make it back in one piece. About four-thirty on the day we left, there was an ice storm near Calgary which turned the highway into a sheet of ice. Little we knew that it would take us four hours to get through the city! Never I have been in such a colossal traffic jam. By the time we got off the freeway, it was eleven-thirty at night, and the kids were crying. We stopped at a motel to try to get a room. They were full up, but when we asked the proprietors if just we could spend the night in their lobby, they took pity on us and made us up a bed in their living room. People can be so kind sometimes. Never again I will think twice about helping people when they need it.

By the next morning, the roads had been cleared, and we made it safely back to Edmonton.

So, that's all for now. Thanks again.

Love,

Barb

V. *Punctuate the following sentences, which form a narration, with commas or semicolons. Do not add periods or capital letters.*

1. Jeff and Jackie Donovan felt that their children were watching too much television**,** but they didn't know what to do about the problem.
2. They tried combinations of threats, punishments, and rewards however, nothing seemed to work.
3. Jeff and Jackie both got home about 5:30 P.M. and they needed to occupy the children's attention while they were fixing dinner.
4. Though they felt so much TV watching wasn't good they allowed it because they had no alternative.
5. Their children weren't getting enough exercise also, they weren't interacting with the neighborhood children.
6. Since a lot of their neighbors were having the same problem with their children someone came up with the idea of starting a neighborhood activities club.
7. The club met every afternoon from 5:00 until 6:30 and two parents from different families supervised activities.
8. The club has been a big success none of the children have watched very much television lately.

VI. *Each of the following sentences has four underlined words or phrases. The four underlined parts of each sentence are marked A, B, C, or D. Circle the letter of the one underlined word or phrase that is not correct.*

1. By (A) pool (B) the world's food supply, we might conceivably (C) avert starvation—provided that (D) the food were disbursed evenly. **A (B) C D**
2. To feel (A) that pleas to sponsor orphans in Third World nations were only (B) rip-off schemes, I refused until (C) recently even (D) to consider giving money. **A B C D**
3. Drivers should be extremely (A) careful when (B) give (C) a ride to hitchhikers, even if (D) they look completely respectable. **A B C D**
4. Although (A) his prose is dense, columnist James Makela, having written (B) in the *Carson City Courier,* forcefully (C) makes the point that only rarely is capital punishment (D) carried out in an evenhanded manner. **A B C D**
5. Automobiles certainly (A) cause many problems, however (B) they fortunately (C) provide us with benefits also (D). **A B C D**
6. Feeling (A) that the subject was beneath me, I unfortunately (B) learned something (C) at all when (D) I took calculus last quarter. **A B C D**
7. Happily (A), the leaders of almost (B) all world nations seem to have realized that something must quickly (C) be done controlling (D) the growth of population. **A B C D**
8. My having landed (A) at Orly Airport, a taxi took me (B) speedily (C) to the hotel where (D) the conference was to be held. **A B C D**

From Grammar to Writing

Sentences and Fragments

1.

As you have learned, a sentence must have at least one independent, or main, clause. (See From Grammar to Writing after Part I, page 46, for a discussion of the sentence.) If a group of words does not have an independent clause, it is a fragment, not a sentence.

> We need to do something about violence. (sentence—independent clause)
> Because it's tearing apart the fabric of societies everywhere. (fragment—dependent clause)
> Sitting in my auto (fragment—no independent clause)

For correctness in writing, we normally avoid sentence fragments. To correct a fragment, we often attach it to an independent clause. We can do this with the fragment above.

> We need to do something about violence **because it's tearing apart the fabric of societies everywhere.**

If there is no independent clause nearby, we can correct a fragment by adding a subject and its verb.

> Interviewed by our news team. (fragment)
> **One commuter was interviewed** by our news team. (sentence)

A. *In the following sentences, underline dependent clauses once and independent clauses twice. Do not underline phrases. In the blank to the left of each item, write* S *for sentence or* F *for fragment.*

__S__ 1. Though you handled the car well, you ran a red light.
______ 2. As soon as you learn the hand signals.
______ 3. Although China is overpopulated, it is trying to correct the problem.
______ 4. We don't solve the problem of violence until we control guns.
______ 5. If a young basketball player from Nigeria can get a scholarship.
______ 6. Because I was one of those students.
______ 7. The economy is perhaps too dependent on the automobile.
______ 8. Carried out right, this procedure would cause the population to stabilize.
______ 9. By the time the train finally arrived in Santa Maria.
______ 10. We need to make some personal sacrifices if we want to help.

B. *Read the following paragraph. Correct the fragments by joining them to the independent clauses to which they are logically connected. Where necessary, add commas and change capitalization, but do not add words.*

The life of Dorothy and Patrick has improved immeasurably\ Since they both got new jobs. Dorothy got a position as a proofreader and editor at a publishing company. That is pioneering new workplace methods. Patrick was hired as a full-time consultant for an engineering firm. The difference between their new jobs and their old ones can be summed up in one word:

flextime. Until they secured these new positions. Dorothy and Patrick had a very difficult time raising their two small children. Their life was extremely stressful. Because they were at the mercy of a nine-to-five schedule and had to pay a lot for day care. In order to get to work on time. They had to have the children at the day care center by 7:30 every morning. Both of their new companies, however, offer a flextime schedule. As long as Dorothy and Patrick put in their forty hours a week. They are free to work. When it is convenient for them. Now they can take turns staying home with the children, and day care is just a memory. Best of all, the children are much happier. Because they are getting the attention they need.

2.

If a sentence has only one clause, it is called a simple sentence.

> I bought a new car last month. (simple sentence: one independent clause)

If two independent clauses are connected by a coordinating conjunction (*and, but, or, nor, for, so, yet*), the larger sentence is called a compound sentence. We place a comma before the coordinating conjunction.

> The tea was virtually flavorless. The sandwich tasted like cardboard.
> The tea was virtually flavorless**, and** the sandwich tasted like cardboard.

We don't normally place a comma before a coordinating conjunction if it does not connect two independent clauses.* That is, there must be a subject and its verb in both clauses.

> We can go out to a film or stay home and watch television.
> (There is no subject in the second half of the sentence.)

Note, though, that if we join two very short independent clauses with a coordinating conjunction, we can eliminate the comma before the coordinating conjunction.*

> I love movies but I hate television.

If a sentence contains an independent clause and one or more dependent clauses, it is called a complex sentence. If the dependent clause comes first, we frequently put a comma after it. If it comes second, we usually don't put a comma before it unless the dependent clause establishes a contrast.

> **Because they provide activity,** school sports are worthwhile.
> School sports are worthwhile **because they provide activity.**
>
> **Though they aren't everything,** jobs are important.
> Jobs are important**, though they aren't everything.**
> (The subordinating conjunction **though** establishes a contrast, so we use a comma before it.)

*Remember that you can, however, use a comma before a coordinating conjunction when it is being used before the last item in a series: I don't like pie, cake**, or** ice cream.

C. *Place commas wherever possible in the following sentences. In the blank to the left of each item, write* S *for a simple sentence,* CPD *for a compound sentence, or* CX *for a complex sentence.*

CPD 1. Violence exists nearly everywhere in the world, and it is spreading.
_______ 2. Since we usually watch TV at home in our living room a TV show doesn't seem like a special event.
_______ 3. The population will continue to increase but natural resources won't.
_______ 4. We must make trains viable again if we expect people to use them.
_______ 5. I listened politely for a while and then excused myself.
_______ 6. The governor isn't in favor of higher taxes nor does she encourage the development of mass transit.
_______ 7. We don't have to buy a lot of groceries at once for we can always stop at the supermarket on the way home from work.
_______ 8. You passed your driving exam with flying colors though you could use some practice in parallel parking.
_______ 9. As I was entering the dining car a violent lurch of the train threw me to the left.

3.

Coordinating conjunctions, subordinating conjunctions, and transitions often have similarities in meaning but are used with different sentence patterns and punctuation. Notice the use of *but*, *although*, and *however* in the following sentences:

> Cars provide many benefits, **but** they also do considerable harm.
> **Although** cars provide many benefits, they also do considerable harm.
> Cars provide many benefits; **however**, they also do considerable harm.

The meanings of these three examples are similar, but the emphasis is different. It is also correct to use a period and a capital letter in the third example:

> Cars provide many benefits**. H**owever, they also do considerable harm.

D. *For each of the following sentences, write two other sentences that express a similar meaning, using the connectors given.*

I tried to board the train and find a seat; however, there wasn't one available.

1. (but) I tried to board the train and find a seat, but there wasn't one available.

2. (although) ____________________

Heavy rail tracks are already there, so heavy rail has gotten the best press.

3. (because) ____________________

4. (therefore) ____________________

You ran a red light, in addition to the fact that you don't seem to know the hand signals.

5. (and) ____

____

6. (also) ____

____

PART VI

Adjective Clauses

UNIT 16

Adjective Clauses: Review and Expansion

INTRODUCTION

Read and listen to an excerpt from the script of a student's speech to a class.

Questions to Consider

1. Are you an "extrovert" or an "introvert"?
2. Is it a good idea to classify people into personality types? Why or why not?

What Type Are You?

Are you a person **who acts on the world,** or are you someone **who lets the world act on you?** Today I'm going to tell you about various categories **that have been developed to classify people.** My hope is that you'll be able to learn something about yourself.

Let's start with the most familiar of the traditional types, the extrovert and the introvert. Many people think that an extrovert is a person **who is courageous, outgoing, and not at all shy.** They believe that an introvert is someone **who is shy, retiring, and fearful.** These are misconceptions. Actually, psychologists define an extrovert as a person **who needs the company of others to become energized,** while an introvert is the kind of person **who needs to be alone to become energized.** Let me illustrate with some examples.

Samantha is actually a shy person **whom others probably wouldn't consider extroverted.** However, Samantha opens up in situations **in which she starts to feel relaxed and appreciated.** At a large party **where she doesn't know many people,** she's shy at first, but when the number of guests thins down, Samantha comes alive. She likes to talk once she finds a group **she feels comfortable with,** and when she opens up she's the kind of person **others find interesting and stimulating.** By eleven o'clock in the evening, she's just getting warmed up. The later it gets, the more animated and activated she starts to feel. Samantha needs others to help energize her, **which is why she is to be considered an extrovert.**

Bill, on the other hand, is someone **whom everyone considers bold, outgoing, the antithesis of shy.** Bill goes to a party and has a good time for a while, but he usually stays only for a short time, for he's a person **whose energies need solitude for replenishment.** He often finds the conversation around him interesting, but he is just as likely to be remembering a time **when he was hiking alone in the mountains or strolling in solitude along the ocean shore.** He needs to be alone to reenergize, **which is why he is to be regarded as an introvert.** By 9:30, Bill is tired and has had enough of the party. He wants to go home and settle down with a good book.

There's a third category **many of us may fall into:** that of the ambivert. Mary, **who is energized sometimes by others and sometimes by being alone,** is a good example. There are times **when Mary is like Samantha.** She gets activated by the stimulation of others and becomes quite outgoing. But there are other times **when Mary is much more like Bill.** On certain Friday nights, for example, after a long, hard workweek, Mary likes nothing better than to spend a quiet evening at home, reading or working on her own projects. Many of us, perhaps even the majority, are probably ambiverts.

Adjective Clauses: Review and Expansion

IDENTIFYING ADJECTIVE CLAUSES

WHO

Are you a person **who acts on the world?**

THAT

I'm going to describe some categories **that have been developed to classify people.**

WHOM

Samantha is a person **whom others wouldn't consider extroverted.**

WHEN

There are times **when many of us feel extroverted** and other times **when we feel introverted.**

(continued on next page)

WHERE

She feels shy at a party **where she doesn't know many people.**

WHICH

A cocktail party is a setting **which can be threatening to a shy person.**

WHOSE

Bill is a person **whose energies need solitude for replenishment.**

PREPOSITION + *WHICH*

Harriet opens up in situations **in which she starts to feel relaxed and appreciated.**

PREPOSITION + *WHOM*

The Grants are the couple **with whom we are negotiating.**

DELETED RELATIVE PRONOUN

Harriet likes to talk once she finds a group **[that] she feels comfortable with.**

NONIDENTIFYING ADJECTIVE CLAUSES

WHO

Meredith, **who is energized sometimes by others and sometimes by being alone,** is an ambivert.

WHOM

The Ochoas, **whom you met at Jason's party,** are really very amiable people.

WHICH

Introversion, **which is a common behavior pattern,** isn't necessarily accompanied by shyness.

WHOSE

Luis, **whose brother is visiting from New York,** does not want to come to the party.

NONIDENTIFYING ADJECTIVE CLAUSE MODIFYING AN ENTIRE PRECEDING AREA

WHICH

Samantha needs others to help energize her, **which is why she is to be considered an extrovert.**

Grammar Notes

1. Adjective clauses are dependent clauses that modify nouns and pronouns. They are introduced by the relative pronouns *who, whom, whose, that,* and *which,* or by *when* and *where.* Sentences with adjective clauses can be seen as a combination of two sentences.

   The man lives across the street from me. The man is the mayor.
   The man **who lives across the street from me** is the mayor.

2. Adjective clauses which are used to identify (distinguish one person or thing from another) are called identifying (or restrictive, defining, or essential).

   A person **who is energized by others** is an extrovert. (The clause, **who is energized by others,** identifies which kind of person is an extrovert.)

   An adjective clause which is not used to identify something but simply adds extra information is called nonidentifying (or nonrestrictive, nondefining, or nonessential).

   Mary, **who sometimes likes to be with others and sometimes likes to be alone,** is an ambivert. (The adjective clause, **who sometimes likes to be with others and sometimes likes to be alone,** is not used to identify the person we are talking about; the name **Mary** identifies the person. The clause gives additional information about Mary.)

   Punctuation note: Nonidentifying adjective clauses are enclosed by commas. Identifying adjective clauses have no commas around them.

   See From Grammar to Writing after Part VI, pages 248 and 249, for more information about punctuation of adjective clauses.

   Pronunciation note: In speech, identifying clauses have no pauses before or after them. Nonidentifying clauses do have a pause before and after them.

   identifying adjective clause
   My sister **who won the lottery** is an unemployed social worker. (I have more than one sister. One of them won the lottery.)

   nonidentifying adjective clause
   My sister, (PAUSE) **who won the lottery,** (PAUSE) is an unemployed social worker. (I have one sister. She won the lottery.)

3. Like all clauses, adjective clauses contain subjects and verbs. The relative pronouns *who, which*, and *that* are used as subjects.

   A person **who tells jokes** is an amusing person. (**Who** is the subject of the clause verb **tells.**)
   The house **that has been condemned** will be bulldozed. (**That** is the subject of the clause verb **has been condemned.**)
   The building **which was damaged by the earthquake** was later demolished by the wrecking crew. (**Which** is the subject of the clause verb **was damaged.**)

   Be careful! Do not use a subject pronoun in an adjective clause in which the relative pronoun is the subject.

   The man **who lives down the street from me is a spelunker.** NOT ~~The man who he lives down the street from me is a spelunker.~~

4. The relative pronouns *whom, that,* and *which* are used as objects in adjective clauses.

   Bill, **whom** many regard as outgoing, is an introvert. (The relative pronoun **whom** is the direct object of the verb **regard.**)
   Samantha likes talking to people **that** she feels comfortable with. (The relative pronoun **that** is the object of the preposition **with.**)

(continued on next page)

The city **which** I find most interesting is Paris. (The relative pronoun **which** is the direct object of the verb **find.**)

Be careful! It is common in conversation to omit the relative pronoun *who, whom, which,* or *that*. This can only be done, however, if the relative pronoun is an object. You cannot omit the relative pronoun if it is the subject of a clause.

may be omitted

The woman **(that/who/whom)** I saw at the carnival is Bill's aunt. (The relative pronouns **that, who,** or **whom** can be omitted because they are objects.)

may not be omitted

A person **who** will help the needy is a caring person. NOT ~~A person will help the needy is a caring person.~~ (The relative pronoun **who** cannot be omitted because it is the subject of the clause.)

Also, you cannot omit a relative pronoun in a nonidentifying adjective clause.

Mary, **who sometimes likes to be alone,** also likes to go to parties. NOT ~~Mary, sometimes likes to be alone, also likes to go to parties.~~

5. Note that *who* and *whom* are used to refer to persons, not things. *That* can be used to refer both to persons and things and is considered more informal than *who* and *whom. Which* is used to refer only to things.

The lady **who/that** stopped by is the president of the Women's Club. NOT ~~The lady which stopped by is the president of the Women's Club.~~

Which and *that* are used interchangeably in identifying clauses.

The house **which/that** is on the corner is for sale.

In a nonidentifying clause, only *which* can be used.

Victoria, **which** is the capital of British Columbia, resembles an English city. NOT ~~Victoria, that is the capital of British Columbia, resembles an English city.~~

6. *Whom* is considerably more formal than *who* and is appropriate for formal writing and careful speech. *Who* is appropriate elsewhere. (Although *who* is used as a subject in adjective clauses, it is often used as an object in conversational speech.)

The people **whom we saw on our vacation** are from Manitoba. (very formal)
The people **who we saw on our vacation** are from Manitoba. (less formal, conversational—**who** used as object)

7. In conversation and informal writing, native speakers commonly place the preposition in an adjective clause at the end of the sentence, and they often omit the relative pronoun.

Samantha likes people she feels comfortable with.

Here are more formal equivalents of this sentence:

Samantha likes people **that she feels comfortable with.** (slightly more formal)
Samantha likes people **who she feels comfortable with.** (a bit more formal)
Samantha likes people **whom she feels comfortable with.** (even more formal)
Samantha likes people **with whom she feels comfortable.** (the most formal)

8. The relative pronoun *whose* is used to introduce an adjective clause in which a possessive is needed. *Whose* does not appear without a following noun in an adjective clause.

The family **whose dog escaped and bit the children** have to pay a fine.

9. Adjective clauses can be introduced with *when* and *where*. Adjective clauses with *when* describe a time; those with *where* describe a place.

Kelly is remembering a time **when life was hard for her.**
Owen feels nervous at parties **where he doesn't know anyone.**

10. The relative pronoun *which* can be used informally to introduce a clause that modifies an entire preceding idea. In these instances, *which* must be preceded by a comma.

I've discovered that Sam is actually quite a shy person, **which surprises me.**

The clause *which surprises me* modifies the entire preceding idea, that Sam is actually quite a shy person. Clauses of this type are common in conversation. They are not recommended for more formal speaking and writing, however. To construct the sentence above more formally, find a specific noun that *which* can modify or try to write the sentence in some other way.

I've discovered that Sam is actually quite a shy person, **a fact which** surprises me. (**Which** modifies the noun **fact.**)

I've been surprised to discover that Sam is actually quite a shy person. (recast sentence)

FOCUSED PRACTICE

1. Discover the Grammar

Read the next part of the student's speech on personality types. Underline all the adjective clauses.

Now here's another way of classifying people. In *The Presidential Character,* historian James Barber classifies presidents into four personality types: active-positive, active-negative, passive-positive, and passive-negative. However, Barber's categories might be applied to anyone, not just to presidents. Let's consider each of these.

First, the active-positive person is the type <u>who acts on the world and derives pleasure from doing so.</u> He or she is one whom others regard as a take-charge leader who gets things done. Active-positives are people who regard the world as their oyster. Daniela, who is president of her high school class, doesn't hesitate to use her power, for she is convinced that her actions will lead to developments that benefit everyone.

Second, the active-negative is a person whose behavior is similar to that of the active-positive in the sense of acting on the world. However, active-negatives feel negative about themselves and the world in certain ways. Martin, who is a good example of an active-negative, is like Daniela in that he gets out and does things, but unlike Daniela, he doesn't get much inner satisfaction from doing so, which is surprising, given that he puts a great amount of effort into his work.

Third, the passive-positive is the kind of individual others regard as a "nice person." Mark, who allows the world to act on him, is a good example of a passive-positive. He can't remember a time when he didn't have a lot of friends.

(continued on next page)

However, he's the kind of individual one can easily take advantage of. Partly because he doesn't have a very positive self-image, he's always agreeable, which is what people like about him.

Fourth, passive-negatives are similar to passive-positives in having a negative self-image and in allowing the world to act on them. However, they tend to view the world as a place where unfortunate things are likely to happen. Passive-negatives often try to compensate for the world's unpleasantness by getting involved in service to others and by stressing moral principles. Laura, who is always worried that disaster is just around the corner,is the perfect passive-negative. She's a member of her school's student review board, a disciplinary group that deals with infractions by students.

Are you an introvert, extrovert, or ambivert? Are you active-positive, active-negative, passive-positive, or passive-negative? Take a look in the mirror.

Reference: James David Barber, *The Presidential Character: Predicting Performance in the*

2. People in the Office

Dolores Atwood, a personnel officer for a publishing company, is writing an evaluation of the employees in her department who are being considered for promotion. Write adjective clauses with **which** *to modify entire preceding ideas.*

Personnel Evaluation
Confidential

Elaine Correa has only been with us for a year but is definitely ready for promotion, ___*which is not surprising*___, given the glowing recommendations she got from her last employer.
1. (not/be/surprising)

Burt Drysdale has proven himself to be a team player, ______________, considering the fact that he rubbed everyone the wrong way at first. I do recommend him for promotion.
2. (I/find/somewhat amazing)

Alice Anderdoff, on the other hand, is not performing up to expectations, ______________ because I was the one who recruited her. I don't believe she should be considered for promotion at this time.
3. (bother/me)

Mel Tualapa is a very congenial employee, ______________, but he can't be promoted yet because he's only been with us for six months.
4. (be/what/everyone/like/about him)

Lately, Tom Curran has often been ill and consistently late to work, ______________, because he was such a model employee at first. I don't recommend him at this time.
5. (be/mystifying)

3. Formal and Informal

Read the following two descriptions. The first is a spoken report by a head attorney to her team of lawyers. The second contains the same information but is a formal written description. Complete the conversation with informal adjective clauses, omitting relative pronouns if possible and using contractions. Complete the written piece with formal adjective clauses. Do not omit relative pronouns, and place prepositions at the beginning of clauses in which they occur. Do not use contractions.

Spoken Report

Our client is a guy who's been in trouble (1. have / be / in trouble) for minor offenses, but I don't think he's a murderer, ________ (2. which / be / why) I feel comfortable defending him. He served time in the penitentiary from 1992 to 1994, and according to all the reports he was a person ________ (3. the other prisoners / look up to). Since he got out of jail in 1994, he's had a good employment record with Textrix, an electronics company ________ (4. he / be / working / for). The psychological reports on him show that when he was in prison he was a person ________ (5. the psychiatrists / consider) well balanced and even-tempered, ________ (6. which / be / why) I don't think he's guilty.

Written Report

Our client is a man who has been in trouble (7. have / be / in trouble) for minor offenses, but I do not believe that he is a murderer, ________ (8. a fact / which / make / me) feel comfortable in defending him. He served time in the penitentiary from 1992 to 1994, and according to all the reports he was a person ________ (9. whom / the other prisoners / respect). Since he was released from prison in 1994, he has had a good employment record with Textrix, an electronics company ________ (10. for / which / he / be / working). His psychological profile suggests that when he was in prison he was a person ________ (11. whom / the psychiatrists / consider) well-balanced and even-tempered, ________ (12. evidence / which / make / me) believe that he is not guilty.

4. Editing

Read the letter from a college student to his parents. Find and correct the eight errors in relative pronouns in adjective clauses.

September 28

Dear Mom and Dad,

Well, the first week of college has been hectic, but it's turned out OK. My advisor is a lady who ~~she~~ is also from Winnipeg, so we had something who we could talk about.

Since I haven't decided on a major, she had me take one of those tests show you what you're most interested in. She also had me do one of those personality inventories that they tell you what kind of person you are. According to these tests, I'm a person whom is an extrovert. I also found out that I'm most interested in things involve being on the stage and performing in some way, who doesn't surprise me a bit. I always liked being in school plays, remember? I signed up for two drama courses.

Classes start on Wednesday, and I'm getting to know the other guys which live in my dormitory. It's pretty exciting being here.

Not much else. I'll call in a week or so.

Love,

Al

COMMUNICATION PRACTICE

5. Practice Listening 1

Listen to the conversation. Then listen again and circle the letter of the sentence which correctly describes what you hear on the tape.

1. (a.) Bob took the job because it pays well.
   b. Bob took the job because he likes the work.
2. a. Paperwork makes Bob angry.
   b. The fact that Bob has been assigned to do a lot of paperwork makes him angry.
3. a. Bob is irritated because his co-worker is a passive-aggressive type of person.
   b. Bob is irritated because he wasn't consulted before being assigned to his co-worker.
4. a. Jennifer is surprised that Bob is disgruntled.
   b. Jennifer is surprised that Bob took the job.
5. a. His feelings about his co-workers are making Bob wonder about himself.
   b. The fact that Bob didn't investigate the company is making him wonder about himself.

6. Tape Discussion

How can you get along better with a co-worker you don't like?

7. Practice Listening 2

Read and listen to the following excerpts from a telephone conversation that Al had with his parents. Then circle the letters of the sentences which correctly describe the meanings of certain sentences that you hear on the tape.

1. (a.) There is one supervisor.
   b. There is more than one supervisor.
2. a. All of Al's roommates are from Canada.
   b. Some of Al's roommates are from Canada.
3. a. Al has one English class.
   b. Al has more than one English class.
4. a. Al has one history class.
   b. Al has more than one history class.
5. a. There is one group of girls.
   b. There is more than one group of girls.
6. a. Al has one advisor.
   b. Al has more than one advisor.

8. Small Group Discussion

Do you think that astrology has any validity? Look at the chart and determine your astrological sign according to your date of birth. Divide into groups of four, in which each person has a different astrological sign. Begin by making sentences with adjective clauses about people born under a particular sign. Then discuss whether you think there is any validity to the characterizations.

Example:

1. A Gemini is a person **who was born between May 21 and June 20.** Geminis are supposed to be people **who are of two minds about everything.** They supposedly have trouble making decisions because they can easily see both sides to a question. To a certain degree, I think this is true because it fits me; I always agonize over decisions. In other ways, though, it doesn't. . . .

Aries the Ram (March 21–April 20)
Strong-willed, daring, enthusiastic, good conversationalist

Taurus the Bull (April 21–May 20)
Warm, stubborn, practical, good parent

Gemini the Twins (May 21–June 20)
Quick, possessed of two personalities, energetic, impatient

Cancer the Crab (June 21–July 22)
Emotional, patriotic, fond of change, needs to feel loved

Leo the Lion (July 23–August 22)
Bright, proud, self-confident, frustrated with failure

Virgo the Virgin (August 21–September 22)
Methodical, intellectual, tending toward perfectionism, good in emergencies

Libra the Scales (September 23–October 22)
Peaceloving, artistic, known for balance and fairness, tending toward perfectionism

Scorpio the Scorpion (October 23–November 22)
Powerful, intense, passionate, bullheaded

Sagittarius the Archer (November 23–December 21)
Direct, highly honest, philosophical, impulsive

Capricorn the Goat (December 22–January 22)
Steady, practical, conservative, stubborn

Aquarius the Water Bearer (January 20–February 19)
Generous, creative, humanitarian, soft-spoken

Pisces the Fishes (February 20–March 20)
Sympathetic, generous, dreamy, can be difficult to know

Adapted from Mary-Paige Royer, *Great Mysteries: Astrology* (San Diego: Greenhaven Press, Inc., 1991).

9. Essay

Consider again the personality categories which have been mentioned in this unit and choose the one that you believe fits you the best. Write an essay of from three to five paragraphs, showing why you fit the category. Include several examples from your own experience.

10. Picture Discussion

Look at this picture as a reflection of a time and a place. What was it like? How are the people dressed? How do they relate to each other?

Example:
The woman **who is standing in the center** of the picture is holding her daughter's hand very tightly.

Georges Seurat, French, 1859–1891, *A Sunday on La Grande Jatte*—1884
oil on canvas, 1884–86, 207.5 x 308 cm, Helen Birch Bartlett Memorial Collection, 1926.224.

UNIT 17

Adjective Clauses with Quantifiers; Adjectival Modifying Phrases

INTRODUCTION

Read and listen to the movie review.

Questions to Consider

1. Do you like movies? What do you look for in a movie? Do you see movies primarily for entertainment, or do you want a film to be something more?
2. *Citizen Kane* is a search to unravel the mystery of a man's life. Can a movie do this better than a book?

☆ FLICK PICKS ☆ FLICK PICKS ☆ FLICK PICKS ☆

CITIZEN KANE: *Now More Than Ever*

by Dartagnan Fletcher

With all the hoopla **surrounding the restoration and reissue of the Orson Welles classic movie *Citizen Kane,*** this reviewer thought it was time to put his two cents in. Approaching the writing of this review, I first jotted down twenty reasons why people should see this picture, **all of which I eventually threw away in favor of these four words:** Just go see it. Anyone **really serious about cinema** should know this film.

Citizen Kane, **said to be based loosely on the life and career of newspaper magnate William Randolph Hearst,** stars Orson Welles in the title role of a man who rises from rags to riches and dies in solitude and loneliness. Welles, **also the picture's director and script co-author,** was only twenty-five when he made *Citizen Kane.* The film wasn't very popular when it was first released in 1941; rank-and-file movie-goers, **many of whom probably regarded its subject matter as too grim,** may have wanted something **happier and more upbeat.** The film won only one Oscar, **for best original screenplay.** In the years since, however, *CK*'s reputation has grown steadily, especially with critics, **most of whom regard it as one of the greatest films ever.** Why?

Citizen Kane opens in the bedroom of the dying millionaire businessman, Charles Foster Kane. As a nurse enters the room, we see the camera focus on the lips of Kane, who mutters his last word before dying: "Rosebud." The nurse's report creates a sensation in the press, **some members of which try frenetically to learn about the life of Kane,**

regarded as the quintessential man of mystery. The edi-tor of one newspaper commissions a major investigation. Who or what was Rosebud? A lost love? Someone or something from Kane's childhood? In an attempt to find out, an investigative reporter interviews people **close to Kane during his life, including his business associates, his former best friend, and his second wife.** In a series of flashbacks **starting with Kane's boyhood in Colorado and ending with Kane's death in his lonely Florida mansion,** we learn about the key events of his life.

Citizen Kane has been criticized on the grounds that its plot hinges too much on a mere device, **the search for Rosebud.** I disagree with this criticism. *Citizen Kane* asks some important questions, **among which is this:** What is the measure of a person? Can a single icon, **Rosebud in this case,** symbolize one's life? Or are we all greater than the sum of our parts?

By the way, I must assure my readers that I will not be a member of that group **responsible for destroying the pleasure of many moviegoers by divulging the secret.** No, this reviewer will not reveal Rosebud's identity. The answer to that question is there to be seen by the careful observer, so if you want to know, find out for yourself by going and seeing the movie. Rumor has it, though, that the lines to get into *CK* are long, **in which case you might want to take along a sleeping bag and a picnic lunch.** The wait will be worth it.

Rating: ★★★★ ★ stars out of a possible ★★★★.

Adjective Clauses with Quantifiers; Adjectival Modifying Phrases

ADJECTIVE CLAUSES WITH QUANTIFIERS

Moviegoers, **many of whom love action-adventure,** are fond of the *Indiana Jones* trilogy.
Foreign films, **most of which are unfamiliar to mass audiences,** are getting more popular.
You may have to pay a lot to see a movie at night, **in which case you might try a matinee.**

ADJECTIVAL MODIFYING PHRASES

Filmmakers **responsible for such masterpieces as *2001*** and ***The Deer Hunter*** should be lionized.
The *Star Wars* trilogy, **directed by George Lucas,** is considered science fiction of high quality.
Akira Kurosawa has made many famous films, **including *Rashomon, Throne of Blood,* and *Ran.***

Grammar Notes

1. Certain nonidentifying adjective clauses have the following pattern: quantifier + preposition + relative pronoun *whom* or *which*. These relative pronouns refer to an earlier head noun.

   Moviegoers, **many of whom probably wanted something more upbeat,** didn't particularly care for *Citizen Kane* at first. (**Whom** refers to the head noun **moviegoers.**)

2. Another adjective clause with a preposition is made without a quantifier. Instead, the clause contains just a preposition and a relative pronoun.

   Citizen Kane asks some important questions, **among which is this:** . . .

   Sentences containing nonidentifying clauses with *of whom* and *of which* are rather formal and more common in writing than in speech.

   Sometimes a noun is used instead of a quantifier.

   Comedies, **examples of which** are *Beverly Hills Cop* and *Home Alone,* continue to be popular.

   Be careful! Remember that we use *whom* to refer to people and *which* to refer to things.

3. The adjective phrase *in which case* is used to introduce a clause. Use this phrase when you could restate the phrase by saying *in that case, in that situation, if that is the case,* or *if that happens.* The relative pronoun *which* refers to an idea described earlier in the sentence.

   Rumor has it that lines to get into the movie are long, **in which case** you should take along a sleeping bag and a picnic lunch. (**In which case** can be restated as "If it is the case that the lines are long . . .")

4. Remember that a phrase is a group of words which doesn't have a subject and a verb. Adjective clauses, both identifying and nonidentifying, are often reduced to adjectival modifying phrases. Speakers and writers do this when they want to achieve an economy of language while maintaining clarity of meaning.

   Anyone **who is serious about cinema** should know this film.
   Anyone **serious about cinema** should know this film. (The relative pronoun **who** and the verb **is** are deleted, leaving an identifying phrase modifying **anyone.**)

   Welles, **who was also the picture's director and script coauthor,** was only twenty-five when he made *Citizen Kane.*
   Welles, **also the picture's director and script coauthor,** was only twenty-five when he made *Citizen Kane.* (The relative pronoun **who** and the verb **was** are deleted, leaving a nonidentifying phrase modifying **Welles.**)

5. There are two ways of reducing an adjective clause to an adjective phrase.

   a. If the adjective clause contains a form of the verb *be*, you can usually delete the relative pronoun, the form of *be*, and any accompanying auxiliaries.

   Citizen Kane, ~~which is~~ **said to be based on the life of William Randolph Hearst,** was released in 1941.
   I'll will not be part of that group of critics ~~who have been~~ **responsible for revealing the identify of Rosebud.**

   b. If the adjective clause does not contain a form of the verb *be*, you can usually delete the relative pronoun and change the verb to its present participial form.

   Charles Foster Kane had a career **that lasted forty years.**

   BECOMES

   Charles Foster Kane had a career **lasting forty years.** (The relative pronoun **that** is deleted, and the simple past tense verb **lasted** is changed to its present participial form.)

6. You can also combine two complete sentences by converting one of the sentences into an adjective phrase.

Ten movies were screened at the festival. They **included** *The Deer Hunter, Ran, 2001, La Dolce Vita,* and *Sweetie.*

Ten movies were screened at the festival, **including *The Deer Hunter, Ran, 2001, La Dolce Vita,* and *Sweetie.***

OR

Ten movies, **including *The Deer Hunter, Ran, 2001, La Dolce Vita,* and *Sweetie,*** were screened at the festival.

FOCUSED PRACTICE

1. Discover the Grammar

Read the textbook discussion comparing the mediums of film and television. Underline adjective clauses with the form **quantifier + preposition + relative pronoun.** *Circle adjective phrases that could have been reduced from clauses.*

A recent survey asked one thousand people this question: Is a film (seen in a movie theater) basically the same as one seen on TV? The participants in the survey, most of whom answered yes to the question, were selected from a variety of ethnic and occupational groups in several countries, including the United States, Canada, Mexico, and Japan. Their responses illustrate the blurring of the perception of differences between the two mediums. Actually, however, film and television are quite dissimilar.

Canadian Marshall McLuhan, regarded as an expert in the field of mass media, is probably the person most responsible for redirecting our thinking about mediums of communication, especially television.

According to McLuhan, the images seen on a screen in a movie theater and on a TV set are fundamentally different. In a theater, projectors shine light through a series of transparent, moving celluloid frames, each of which contains a separate photograph. The image projected on the screen is essentially solid.

On a television screen, however, the image, composed of millions of dots, is not solid but representational. The human brain must perceive the pattern of dots and mentally convert it into pictures. Film, says McLuhan, is a "hot" medium, while television is a "cool" medium requiring more mental energy. Over the years, legions of people have railed against television, convinced that it leads to mental laziness. McLuhan would apparently disagree. His theory gives a plausible explanation for a frequent complaint by TV viewers, many of whom report an almost irresistible tendency to fall asleep while watching television. Their brains have to work harder to perceive the image.

2. Film Trivia

Complete the following statements about movies, writing adjective clauses in the form **quantifier + preposition + relative pronoun.**

1. Jack Lemmon and Walter Matthau, both of whom starred in The Odd Couple, also acted together in *The Fortune Cookie, The Front Page,* and *JFK.*
   (both / star / in *The Odd Couple*)
2. Sean Connery, Roger Moore, and Timothy Dalton, ______________________, come from Britain.
   (all / have / play / the role of James Bond)
3. *Star Wars, The Empire Strikes Back,* and *Return of the Jedi,* ______________________, are the middle three films in a projected nine-part series.
   (all / have / earn / over $100 million)
4. *Throne of Blood* and *Ran,* ______________________, are based on Shakespearean plays.
   (both / direct / by Akira Kurosawa)
5. Walt Disney's animated productions, ______________________, are known worldwide.
   (most / be / loved by children)
6. Lina Wertmüller and Wim Wenders, ______________________, are both highly regarded European film directors.
   (neither / be / well known to American mass audiences)

3. Popular Movies

Complete each sentence with a nonidentifying adjective phrase for each film mentioned.

1. *E.T.,* directed by Steven Spielberg, was the top-earning film until it was toppled by Spielberg's own dinosaur opera.
   (direct / by / Steven Spielberg)
2. *Jurassic Park,* ______________________, is the biggest single moneymaking film of all time.
   (base / on / Michael Crichton's novel)
3. *Grease,* ______________________, is the top-grossing musical film with live actors.
   (star / John Travolta and Olivia Newton-John)
4. *Dances with Wolves,* ______________________, is the top-grossing western film.
   (direct and produce / by / Kevin Costner)
5. The *Star Wars* trilogy, ______________________, was conceived, written, and produced by George Lucas.
   (feature / Harrison Ford, Carrie Fisher, and Mark Hamill)

4. Movie Genres

Combine each pair of sentences about types of movies into a single sentence with an adjective clause or phrase.

1. Many recent science fiction films have been huge financial successes. They include the *Star Wars* trilogy, *Close Encounters of the Third Kind*, and the *Terminator* movies.

   Many recent science fiction films, including the Star Wars trilogy, Close Encounters of the Third Kind, and the Terminator movies, have been huge financial successes.

2. Westerns have been making a comeback in recent years. Examples of them are *Dances with Wolves, Unforgiven,* and *Wyatt Earp*.

3. Musical animated films have also become very popular. They include *Aladdin, The Lion King,* and *Beauty and the Beast.*

4. It looks as though sequels to big movie hits may lose their appeal. In that case, moviemakers will be forced to become more creative.

5. Editing

Read the letter. Find and correct the ten errors involving adjective clauses and phrases. Delete verbs or change relative pronouns where necessary, but do not change punctuation or add relative pronouns.

Malibu Manor
Bed and Breakfast

July 15

Dear John,

Diana and I are having a great time in Los Angeles. We spent the first day at the beach in Venice and saw where Harry and Tonto was filmed—you know, that movie ~~starred~~ starring Art Carney and an orange cat? Yesterday we went to Universal Studios and learned about all the cinematic tricks, most of them I wasn't aware of. Amazing! The funny thing is that, even though you know that an illusion is presented on the screen is just an illusion, you still believe it's real when you see the movie.

Then we took the tram tour around the premises and saw several actors working, some of them I recognized. I felt like jumping off the tram and shouting, "Would everyone is famous please give me you autograph?" In the evening we went to a party at the home of one of Diana's friends, many of them are connected with the movie business. I had a really interesting conversation with a fellow works in the industry who claims that a lot of movies are made these days are modeled conceptually after amusement park rides. Just like the rides, they start slowly and easily, then they have a lot of twists and turns are calculated to scare you to death, and they end happily. Pretty fascinating, huh? What next?

Sorry to babble on so much about movies, but you know what an addict I am. Anyway, I may be coming back a day early, in that case I'll call and let you know so that you can pick me up at the airport.

Love you lots,

Jean

COMMUNICATION PRACTICE

6. Practice Listening

Listen to the TV film reviewer give her weekly review. Then listen again to certain of the reviewer's sentences. For each numbered item, respond true (T) *or false* (F) *to indicate if it correctly restates the sentence that you hear on the tape.*

__T__ 1. The film festival can be seen this holiday weekend.

______ 2. None of these great movies have been seen in movie theaters in more than a decade.

______ 3. *My Life as a Dog* was created by Lasse Hallström, a Swedish director.

______ 4. In *My Life as a Dog,* a young boy sends his confused dog to his unhappy relatives in the country.

______ 5. In *The Discreet Charm of the Bourgeoisie,* hilarious, unsuccessful, middle-class French people try to get together for dinner.

______ 6. *The Deer Hunter* starred Michael Cimino.

______ 7. *The Deer Hunter* makes the reviewer cry.

______ 8. Jeff Bridges was responsible for launching *The Last Picture Show.*

______ 9. Black-and-white movies are not pretty.

______ 10. All who regard themselves as serious movie junkies must see *Casablanca.*

7. Group Discussion

Divide into groups of six to eight and discuss one of the following topics. Prepare carefully for the discussion by doing some research. Share the main points of your discussion with the class as a whole.

Topic 1. The rating system for films should be strengthened/should be left as it is.
Topic 2. Movies have/have not become too violent.
Topic 3. In general, "Hollywood" films are/are not inferior to European and Asian films.

8. Essay

Write your own movie review in an essay of three to five paragraphs. Choose a film that you liked or disliked, but try to be objective in your review.

9. Picture Discussion

Look at this picture for a few minutes. Take note of the details. Remember as best as you can the location and the description of the people in the scene. Then, with a partner and with books closed, discuss all the details you can remember. When you have finished, open your books and discuss how accurate you were.

Example:
The man **holding the paintbrush** might be the artist who painted this picture.

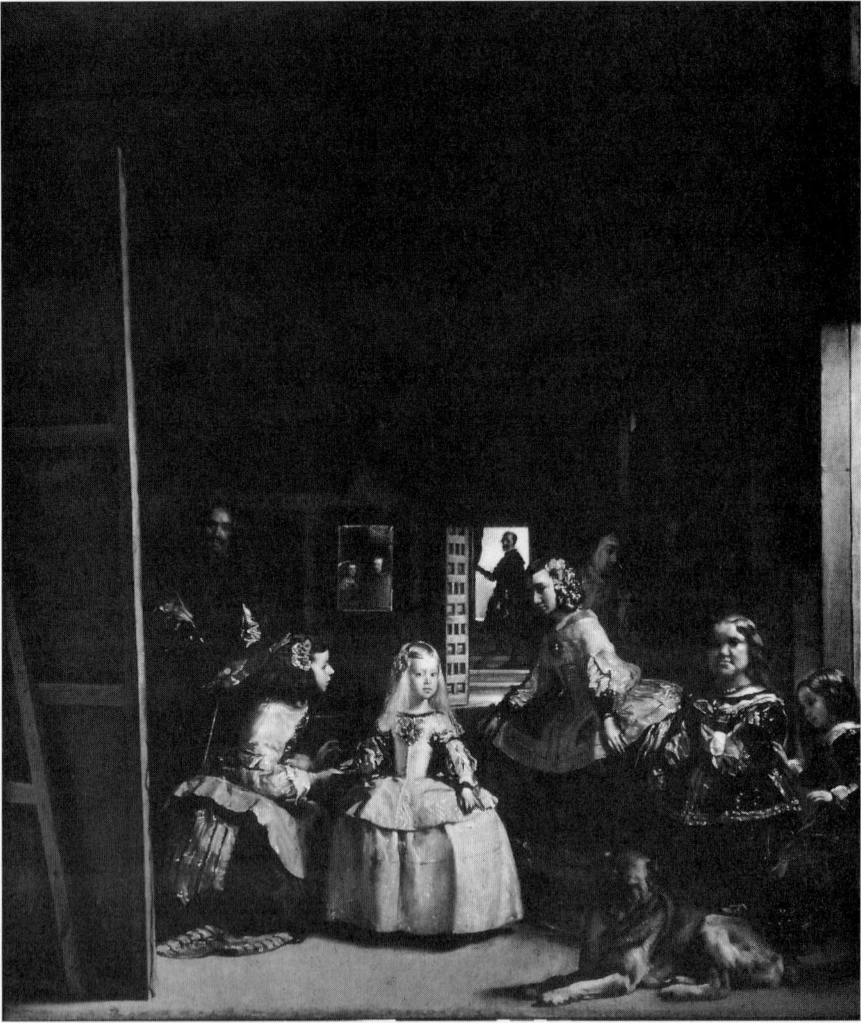

Diego Velázquez, *Las meninas.* Prado, Madrid, Spain. Giraudon/Art Resource, NY *(The Maids of Honor)*

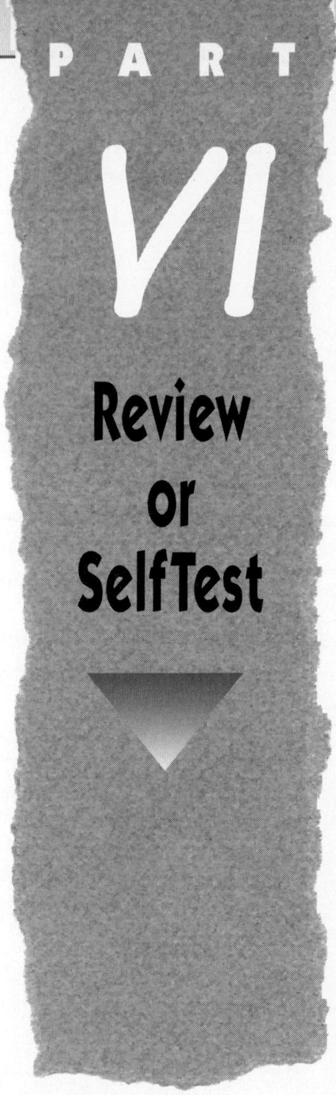

I. *Read the text and underline all of the adjective clauses.*

Recently at work I had an experience that proved to me the truth of that old adage: Things may not be what they seem. The experience involved two people I work with in my secretarial job. The first, whom I'll call "Jennifer," is one of those sunny types who always greet you in a friendly manner and never have an unkind word to say. The second, whom I'll call "Myrtle," is the type who rarely gives compliments and can sometimes be critical. Between the two of them, I thought Jennifer was the one who was my friend. Myrtle never seemed to care much for me, which is why I didn't seek out her friendship. I learned, though, that I had been reading them wrong.

About two months ago, some money was stolen from someone's purse in the office. It happened on an afternoon when all three of us, Jennifer, Myrtle, and I, were working together. Our boss, who tends to jump to conclusions, questioned the three of us and said that someone whose name he wouldn't reveal had implicated me in the theft. Jennifer, whom I expected to stand up for me, hemmed and hawed and said she didn't know where I'd been at the time of the theft, which was a lie. Myrtle, however, spoke up and said she knew I couldn't have been the one who had stolen the money because she and I had been working together all afternoon. The boss accepted her statement, and that ended the unpleasantness. It also ended my friendship with Jennifer. I found out later that she wanted my job. I don't know whether or not she was the one who took the money, but I do know that the old proverb that tells us not to judge a book by its cover has some truth in it. Myrtle and I have been friends ever since.

II. *Read the sentences, which form a narration. Circle the correct relative pronoun for each sentence.*

1. David and Rebecca Carter, that/who got married about a year ago, recently bought a new house.
2. The neighborhood in that/in which they have been living is a somewhat dangerous one.
3. The neighborhood that/who they are moving into is much safer.
4. Their new house, that/which they bought quite cheaply, does need some fixing up.
5. However, they will be receiving some help from their neighbors, most of who/most of whom they like.
6. The Rossis, who/whom live next door to them, have volunteered to lend their tools.
7. The Roybals, who/whom live across the street from David and Rebecca, have promised to help them put in a new lawn.
8. The Rossis, who/whose daughter is the same age as Mackenzie, David and Becky's daughter, are helping Mackenzie make new friends.
9. Rebecca, that/who works for a county hospital, will still have to commute to work.
10. David, whom/whose company is nearby, will be able to walk to work.

III. *Read the sentences, which form a narration. Put the relative pronoun in parentheses if it can be omitted. Do not omit relative pronouns if they are subjects.*

1. On our trip to Europe last summer, we met a lot of people (whom) we liked.
2. One of the most interesting was a young man from Spain who was named Jaime.
3. We were hitchhiking outside Madrid. Jaime, who was on his way home from Seville, stopped and picked us up.
4. The car that he was driving was a 1972 Volkswagen.
5. Jaime took us to his house, which was not far from downtown Madrid, and invited us to stay for a few days.
6. He also introduced us to a group of people that we felt very comfortable with.
7. We were scheduled to go to Portugal next, so Jaime gave us the address of a cousin of his who lived in Coimbra.
8. We had such a wonderful time in Spain and Portugal that we decided to go back next year, which will cost money but will be worth it.

IV. *Complete each sentence with a nonidentifying* **which** *clause that modifies the first clause. Add necessary pronouns and verbs.*

1. Frannie needs to stay home to reenergize herself, which is why she can be termed an introvert.
   (is / why / can be termed / an introvert)
2. Johnathan becomes energized when he is around other people,
   ______________________________.
   (why / can be termed / an extrovert)
3. Passive-positive people appreciate the approval of others,
   ______________________________.
   (why / often / have many friends)
4. Active-positive people like to make their mark upon the world,
   ______________________________.
   (why / tend / to value accomplishment)
5. Active-negative people tend to have somewhat negative self-images,
   ______________________________.
   (why / not always feel satisfied with their accomplishments)

V. *Each of the following sentences contains four underlined words or phrases, marked A, B, C, or D. Circle the letter of the one underlined word or phrase which is not correct.*

1. Federico Fellini, whose (A) work including (B) *8½, La Dolce Vita,* and *Satyricon* and who (C) is (D) one of the most famous film directors in the world, died in 1993. — A (B) C D
2. Marcello Mastroianni and Sophia Loren, both (A) of which (B) are well known internationally, appeared in certain films directed (C) by Fellini, including (D) *Blood Feud* and *Yesterday, Today, and Tomorrow.* — A B C D

3. Police in Charleston are investigating a crime that
A B
was committing yesterday evening between 11:00 P.M.
C
and midnight at the city art museum, which is located
D
on Fifth Avenue.

A B C D

4. Detective Amanda Reynolds, who is the chief investigating
A
officer in the case, says that the police have no suspects
B
yet but are focusing on tips suggest that the theft may
C D
have been an inside job.

A B C D

5. Al, whom is a freshman at the university, is pleased with
A
his college living situation because he likes the people
B
he is rooming with.
C D

A B C D

6. His courses, none of which are easy, are all classes requiring
A B C
a considerable amount of study, that is why he has joined
D
a study group.

A B C D

7. Textrix, the company for that Alex works, tends to employ
A B
people who are self-starters and who have at least ten years
C D
of experience in the field.

A B C D

8. Alicia, an extrovert loves working with people and can
A B
also work independently, had many accomplishments in her
last job, which is why I think she's the person we should hire.
C D

A B C D

9. The lines to get into *Sweetie*, a film directed by New Zealander
A B C
Jane Campion, may be long, in that case I would recommend
D
going to a matinee screening.

A B C D

10. Jaime, who has been employed for ten years at a company that
A B
stresses team-building and cooperative effort, is a person who
C
has learned to value the people with he works.
D

A B C D

From Grammar to Writing

Punctuation of Adjective Clauses

1.

Review the two types of adjective clauses: identifying and nonidentifying. Identifying adjective clauses identify or give essential information. Nonidentifying clauses give additional or nonessential information.

> I saw three movies last week. The movie **that I liked best** was *Jurassic Park.*

The adjective clause, *that I liked best*, is identifying because it says which movie I am talking about. If the clause were removed, the sentence would not express the same thought.

> The movie was *Jurassic Park.*

Therefore, the clause is essential for the sentence's meaning.

> Casablanca, **which contains the famous song "*As Time Goes By,*"** is considered a film classic.

The nonidentifying clause, *which contains the famous song "As Time Goes By,"* adds more information about *Casablanca*. This clause, however, is not used to identify. If it were removed, the sentence would still make sense.

> *Casablanca* is considered a film classic.

In speech, identifying clauses have no appreciable pauses before or after them. Therefore, they are not enclosed in commas when written. Nonidentifying clauses, on the other hand, do have pauses before and after them. In writing, they must be enclosed in commas.

> A person **who needs others to become energized** is an extrovert. (identifying; no commas)
> James, **who comes alive when he feels comfortable with the people around him,** is an extrovert. (nonidentifying; commas)

If you are unsure whether a clause is identifying or nonidentifying, try reading it aloud. The natural pauses made by your voice will help you to determine whether or not the clause needs to be enclosed in commas.

A. *Punctuate the following sentences with adjective clauses. They form a narration. Do not place commas around clauses that identify.*

1. Tom and Sandra**,** who have been married for more than twenty-five years**,** are both outgoing people.
2. Tom who is clearly an extrovert loves meeting new people.
3. Sandra who is very quick to make friends loves to have friends over for dinner.
4. Tom and Sandra have two married sons both of whom live abroad.
5. The son who is older lives with his family in Britain.
6. The son who is younger lives with his family in southern Italy.
7. Tom and Sandra own a house in the city and one in the country. The one that they spend most of their time in is in the city.
8. The house that they spend summers in is located in Vermont.

2.

Adjective phrases are also identifying or nonidentifying, depending on whether they add essential or extra information.

> The postwar director most responsible for putting Italian cinema on the map is Federico Fellini. (identifying; no commas)
>
> Federico Fellini, the director of such classics as *8½*, died in 1993. (nonidentifying; commas)

B. *Punctuate the following sentences with adjective phrases.*

1. A film produced by George Lucas is almost guaranteed success.
2. A film directed by Steven Spielberg is likely to be a blockbuster.
3. *The Passenger* directed by Michelangelo Antonioni and starring Jack Nicholson is not well known in North America.
4. Many Canadians including Donald Sutherland and Michael J. Fox are major international film stars.
5. The Universal Studios resort located in California was built decades ago.
6. The Universal Studios resort located in Florida was built much more recently.

C. *The following letter from a first-year college student contains a number of identifying and nonidentifying adjective clauses and phrases. Punctuate the letter by adding commas where necessary.*

September 30

Dear Mom and Dad,

Thanks for bringing me down here to the university last Sunday. Classes didn't start until Wednesday, so I had a few days to get adjusted. I'm signed up for five classes: zoology, calculus, English, and two history sections. It's a heavy load, but they're all courses that will count for my degree. The zoology class which meets at 8:00 every morning is going to be my hardest subject. The history class that I have in the morning is on Western Civilization; the one in the afternoon is on early United States history. Calculus which I have at noon every day looks like it's going to be easy. Besides zoology, the other class that's going to be hard is English; we have to do a composition a week.

I like all of my roommates but one. There are four of us in our suite including two girls from Texas and a girl from Manitoba. Sally who is from San Antonio is great; I feel like I've known her all my life. I also really like Anne who is the girl from Manitoba. Heather the other girl from Texas is kind of a pain, though; she's one of those types of people who never tell you what's bothering them and then get hostile. All in all, though, it looks like it's going to be a great year. I'll write again in a week or so.

Love,

Vicky

PART VII

Noun Clauses

UNIT 18

Noun Clauses: Subjects and Objects

INTRODUCTION

Read and listen to Jim Bresler's interview of Zeya Mason, one of the first participants in the recently expanded National Service Program.

Questions to Consider

1. Do you think that all citizens owe their country something?
2. Would you like to participate in some form of national service?

Jim: Zeya, I want to thank you for doing this interview. Do you mind **if I record your answers?**

Zeya: No, I don't mind at all. Go right ahead.

Jim: OK. Zeya, you're one of the very first participants in the program, so here's kind of an obvious first question: Tell me **what you think of National Service.**

Zeya: I think **it's a wonderful program.** It's given me something worthwhile to do, and it's helped me figure out **what my career is going to be.**

Jim: Do you believe **that citizens owe their country something?**

Zeya: I do, yes. The country has given all of us a lot. In return, we all need to do **whatever we can for the country.**

Jim: What are you doing in your National Service assignment?

Zeya: I'm working in a literacy program. I teach people who aren't completely literate how to read and write.

Jim: Are the people you work with immigrants?

Zeya: Some of them are, but others are people who were born in this country. Actually, I'm assigned to work with **whoever needs literacy training**.

Jim: Tell me **what made you decide to join the National Service Program**.

Zeya: Well, I graduated from high school a year ago, and I was going to go right on to college. But after thirteen years of school, I realized **I was tired. What became really clear to me** was the fact that I just wasn't ready for serious study. The National Service Program had just been approved, so I applied and was accepted.

Jim: What do you like about your job?

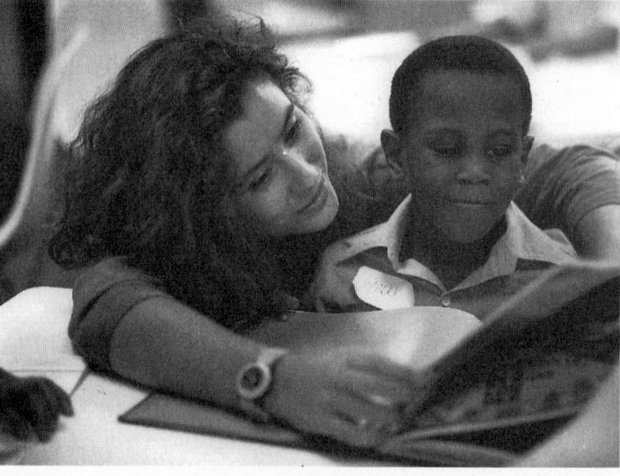

Zeya: Well, corny as it may sound, **the fact that I'm helping others** fulfills me. For instance, I've been working with a forty-seven-year-old lady from Laos; she and her husband came to this country five years ago. She never really learned to read and write, so I was assigned to do **whatever I could to help her**. She's a wonderful lady, and she's made great progress.

Jim: It's admirable that you're helping others, but there must be something else in it for you, some long-term benefits.

Zeya: Oh yes, definitely. By the time I finish my assignment in two years, I'll have earned $5,000 that I can apply to my college education.

Jim: So you do intend to go to college, then?

Zeya: Yes. I don't know **where I'm going,** but I do know **I'll be majoring in education.**

Jim: Great. Zeya, do you think **this program is for everyone?**

Zeya: Well, I don't know **if everyone would be interested,** but I do think **that just about anyone could benefit from it. Whoever isn't going right on to college from high schoo**l ought to give it serious consideration.

Jim: Well, Zeya, thank you again for doing this interview, and good luck in the future.

Zeya: My pleasure.

Noun Clauses: Subjects and Objects

SUBJECT
What became really clear to me was the fact that I wasn't ready for college.
Whoever isn't going right to college should consider National Service.
The fact that I'm helping others fulfills me.

OBJECT
Do you believe **that citizens owe their country something?**
I think **(that) it's a wonderful program.**
Tell me **what you think of National Service.**
We all need to do **whatever we can.**
Do you mind **if I record your answers?**
I don't know **where I'm going to be attending college.**
I'm assigned to work with **whoever needs literacy training.**

Grammar Notes

1. Noun clauses are dependent clauses that perform the same functions that regular nouns do: They can be subjects, direct objects, indirect objects, or objects of prepositions.

   SUBJECT
   What bothers me is his lack of initiative.
   DIRECT OBJECT
   We all need to do **whatever we can.**
   INDIRECT OBJECT
   The program should provide **whoever is unemployed** a two-year job.
   OBJECT OF PREPOSITION
   I'm assigned to work with **whoever needs literacy training.**

   See Unit 19 for a discussion of noun clauses as complements.

2. Noun clauses are often introduced by *what, that, who, whom, where, how, why, whether (or not),* and by the words *whatever, whichever (one), wherever, whoever, whomever, however.*

   What I need is a challenging job.
   Do **what you have to do.**
   Whatever you want to do tonight is all right by me.
   I know **that I'll enjoy National Service.**

   Be careful! Don't confuse *however* as a clause introducer with *however* as a transition word.

   However you finance your college education is up to you. (clause introducer)
   I want to go to college. **However,** I don't know how I'm going to finance it. (transition)

3. Remember the distinction between *who* and *whom, whoever* and *whomever. Who* and *whoever* are used as subjects, while *whom* and *whomever* are used as objects in formal English. Many native speakers don't use *whom* and *whomever.*

SUBJECT VERB
Award the prize to **whoever** comes through the door first. (**Whoever** is the subject of the verb **comes** in the dependent clause.)

OBJECT SUBJECT VERB
Award the prize to **whomever** you like. (**Whomever** is the direct object of the verb **like.**)

Be careful! If you are unsure whether to use *whoever* or *whomever,* be aware that the noun clause (like all clauses) must have both a subject and a verb.

SUBJECT VERB
I'm assigned to work with **whoever** needs literacy training.

In this sentence, the noun clause *whoever needs literacy training* is the object of the preposition *with.* This would seem to require the object form *whomever.* However, the verb in the noun clause *must* have a subject, so *whoever* is the correct choice.

Usage note: Although native speakers often replace *whom* and *whomever* with *who* and *whoever* in conversation or informal writing, in careful speech and formal writing the use of *whom* and *whomever* is recommended.

Appoint **whomever** you like. (formal)
Appoint **whoever** you like. (informal)

4. When a noun clause beginning with *that* functions as a direct object, the word *that* may be omitted.

Do you think **(that) National Service is for everyone?**

5. Noun clauses are sometimes embedded questions with *if* or *whether (or not).*

Do you mind **if I record your answers?**
Do you know **whether or not she has left?**

6. Indirect speech is expressed in noun clauses. Remember to follow the sequence of tenses in changing direct speech to indirect speech.

"Mary, what are you going to be when you grow up?" John asked.
John asked Mary **what she was going to be when she grew up.**

7. Note that a noun clause sometimes includes the phrase *the fact that.*

The fact that I'm helping others fulfills me. (The clause **the fact that I'm helping others** is the subject of the entire sentence.)
I'm bothered by **the fact that I'm not doing anything socially useful.** (The clause **the fact that I'm not doing anything useful** is the object of the preposition **by.**)

FOCUSED PRACTICE

1. Discover the Grammar

Read the editorial, which recently appeared in The Pleasantville Herald. *Underline all noun clauses used as subjects or objects.*

Make National Service Mandatory

Congress recently approved a bill to fund a National Service program, and the president signed it. We think this is a small step in the right direction, but we also believe it doesn't go nearly far enough.

In our view, whoever gets something from the nation should be required to give the nation something in return. Think for a minute about what we receive. We all have access to free education through high school, police protection, national security, roads and highways, national parks—the list goes on and on. We suggest that it is time to reinvoke John F. Kennedy's famous call to action: "Ask not what your country can do for you; ask what you can do for your country."

We propose that Congress pass new legislation creating a job corps and requiring all youths to serve in it. It

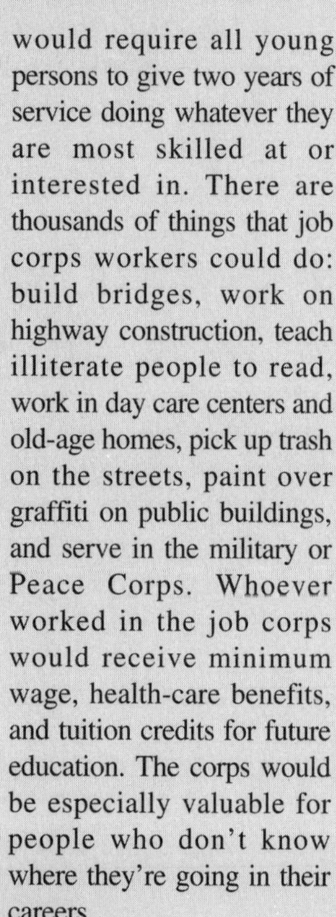

would require all young persons to give two years of service doing whatever they are most skilled at or interested in. There are thousands of things that job corps workers could do: build bridges, work on highway construction, teach illiterate people to read, work in day care centers and old-age homes, pick up trash on the streets, paint over graffiti on public buildings, and serve in the military or Peace Corps. Whoever worked in the job corps would receive minimum wage, health-care benefits, and tuition credits for future education. The corps would be especially valuable for people who don't know where they're going in their careers.

What this country needs is a sense of community and togetherness. Mandatory national service is the way to achieve it.

2. Is There Life After High School?

Two high school seniors are having a conversation about life after graduation. Fill in the blanks in their conversation with clauses from the box.

whoever hires me	if you might have a point
what you're going to do	what I have to do
the army will help me decide	whatever I'm told
I'm going into the army	what I want as a career
I'll get a job	whatever your boss tells you

Colleen: We graduate next month. Do you know ___what you're going to do___ (1.)?

Amanda: I don't have a clue. I guess ________________ (2.).

Colleen: Doing what?

Amanda: Doing ________________ (3.).

Colleen: By whom?

Amanda: By ________________ (4.). What about you?

Colleen: I think ________________ (5.).

Amanda: The army? Why?

Colleen: Well, I don't know yet ________________ (6.). I figure ________________ (7.). Why don't you join along with me?

Amanda: What? And be told ________________ (8.) every minute of the day?

Colleen: You just said you're willing to do ________________ (9.). Anyway, it's not like that. You can learn a lot of new things and get away from home to boot. Think it over.

Amanda: Hmm . . . I wonder ________________ (10.).

3. Reach Out and Help Someone

Two friends in their late twenties, Brady and Pablo, are talking. Fill in the blanks in their conversation with **whatever, whichever, whoever,** *or* **however** *and correct forms of the indicated verbs. You will use some of these words more than once.*

Pablo: What's the matter with you lately? You seem really down in the dumps.

Brady: I don't know. I'm just not very happy. Take girls, for example. ___Whoever I meet___ (1. I / meet) bores me. I'd like to meet some new and interesting people.

Pablo: What about work? Doesn't that satisfy you?

Brady: Nah, I've been there so long that I can do ______________ (2. I / want), but there's no challenge anymore. Right now there are five major projects the company is doing. My boss tells me to work on ______________ (3. one / interest me) the most. The trouble is, none of them interest me.

Pablo: Why don't you try doing some volunteer work? That's what I do—I go down to the community center and work with ______________ (4. need / help) on that day. You get your mind off yourself when you're volunteering.

Brady: What kind of things do you do?

Pablo: Sometimes I just sit and talk to old people. Sometimes I umpire a baseball game. Sometimes I help a kid with his homework. I do ______________ (5. I / can).

Brady: How much time do you have to put in, say, every week?

Pablo: You can put in ______________ (6. much / time / you / want). There are no rules on that.

Brady: OK, so what do I do?

Pablo: Just go down to the community center some evening. Talk to ______________ (7. be) at the main desk. Say you're there to help. You'll do ______________ (8. need / to be done).

Brady: OK, I'll give it a try. Helping others might cheer me up. What's the address?

4. Editing

Read and edit the letter, correcting the seven errors in noun clauses.

September 22

Dear Colleen,

Well, old pal, here I am at Fort Jackson. I have to say you were right about joining the army. I just wish we could have been stationed together. I'll admit ~~what~~ *that* basic training was tough, but now that it's over with, I'm having a great time. Whomever says that you're treated like a slave is wrong. There are rules to follow, but they're not unreasonable. That I like best about my situation is what I get to study whatever I want. I chose telecommunications. I assume that things are the same for you. Is that right?

The other thing what I like about the army, believe it or not, is the social life. In the evenings and on some weekends we're free to spend our time with whomever we want. I've met some interesting women, and there are dances and get-togethers attended by guys from off the base. I met a nice one at the dance last weekend.

I just wonder that I would be doing if I hadn't gone in the army. I hope what things are going as well for you as they are for me. Write soon.

Best,

Amanda

COMMUNICATION PRACTICE

5. Practice Listening

Listen to the conversation between a returned Peace Corps volunteer and a local newspaper reporter who is interviewing her. Then listen again to certain of the sentences in the interview. For each item, circle the letter of the sentence which correctly restates the sentence that you hear.

1. (a.) Describe your Peace Corps experience.
   b. Tell us if you liked the Peace Corps.
2. a. It was the most important experience I've ever had.
   b. I'd have to say that life is an experience. It was the most difficult experience I've ever had.

(continued on next page)

3. a. Describe what the experience did for you.

   b. Describe your job experience.

4. a. We gave medical attention to all people asking for it.

   b. We needed to give medical attention to everyone.

5. a. I especially liked the villagers.

   b. I especially liked the villagers' attitude.

6. a. However, many people would show up at the town hall.

   b. I taught English as a second language to all the people who showed up for it at the town hall.

7. a. What was the most difficult thing about being in the Peace Corps?

   b. What does being in the Peace Corps tell us?

8. a. Loneliness bothered me more than anything else.

   b. Whatever bothered me made me lonely.

9. a. We were allowed a room.

   b. We were allowed to choose a roommate.

10. a. I adjusted to another culture.

    b. I learned about the difficulties of adjusting to another culture.

11. a. Volunteers can use any of the skills they have.

    b. Whatever you can volunteer is a skill.

6. Small Group Discussion

Divide into small groups. Discuss one or more the of the following topics. Share your findings with the other groups.

1. What I want out of life is . . .

   Example:

   A: What I want out of life is a challenging job and a fulfilling relationship with someone.

   B: Tell us **what you would consider a challenging job.**

2. What I find hardest about being an adult is . . .
3. What I find most interesting about being an adult is . . .
4. What this country needs is . . .

7. Debate

Divide into two groups and have a debate on this topic:

The government should (OR shouldn't) require some sort of national service from every citizen.

National Service could be interpreted narrowly to refer to military service only, or it could be interpreted broadly, allowing many options, such as medical service, working with youths, park or conservation service. Whichever side you choose, do some research on the issue and try to include information you might have about national service in other countries.

8. Essay

After you have participated in the debate in exercise 7 on page 260, write an essay in which you clarify your own position. Did the debate change your ideas at all, or is your position basically the same as it was originally?

9. Picture Discussion

Study this picture individually for a few minutes. Jot down your ideas about what happened before this situation and what might happen next.

Example:
What might have happened is . . .
I think . . .

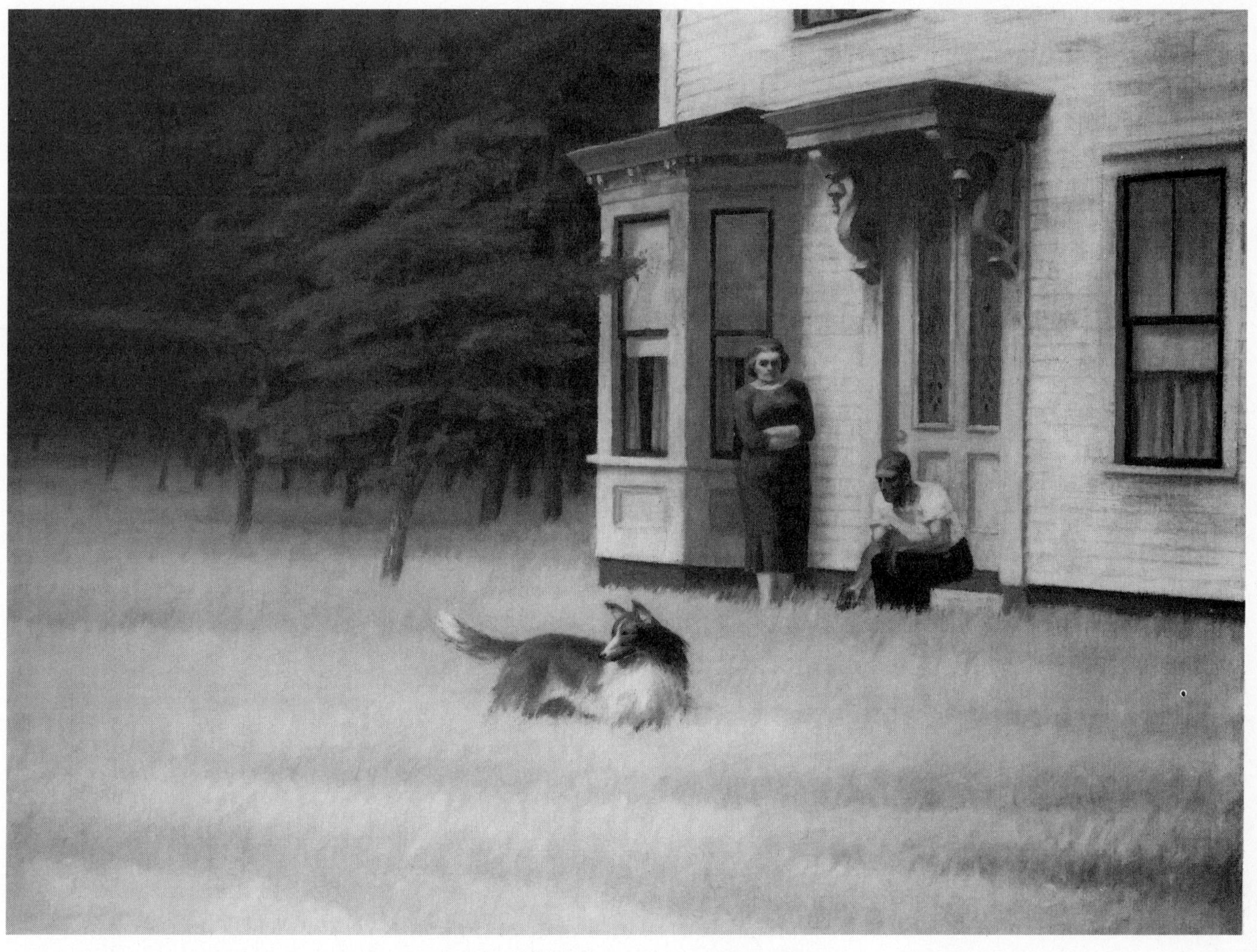

Edward Hopper, *Cape Cod Evening*. (1939)
Oil on canvas, 30 1/4 x 40 1/4". National Gallery of Art, Washington. John Hay Whitney Collection

UNIT 19

Complementation

INTRODUCTION

Read and listen to the radio interview of Dr. Sandra Stalley, an expert on educational problems, about issues in U.S. education.

Questions to Consider

1. What makes a good educational system?
2. Do you know about the educational systems of more than one country? How are they different? How are they the same?

WVIV: Dr. Stalley, recently there's been a lot said and written about the crisis in American education. Is it true **that we're in a crisis?**

Stalley: Yes, it's quite apparent **that education is in a crisis situation in this country.** In fact, it's absolutely astounding **that the system has degenerated so much so quickly.**

WVIV: What would you say are examples of this?

Stalley: Well, for one thing, it's a fact **that more students are dropping out of high school than fifteen or twenty years ago.** For another, it's obvious **that violence has gotten more and more commonplace in schools.** But the most important indicator is **the fact that test scores have dropped and continue to stay low.**

WVIV: But isn't it true **that test scores don't necessarily measure students' knowledge all that well?**

Stalley: There's some truth in that, yes. However, there's no doubt **that American students compare rather poorly with students from other industrialized nations in subjects like science, mathematics, and geography**.

WVIV: What do you think is wrong with our educational system?

Stalley: Well, the fact that many schools are large and impersonal is one thing that's wrong. And it's frequently the case **that there are too many students in individual classes.** Teachers can't do a very effective job if they can't give students individual attention. That kind of job assignment is hard enough on teachers, but it's the students who suffer the most. Another example is **that schools often don't teach students the things they really need to know.** However, the main problem in education is the belief **that the school system is the place to solve most of society's ills.**

WVIV: What do you mean, exactly?

Stalley: Well, it seems pretty clear **that society expects the schools to do just about everything.** Some parents insist **that schools be open early in the morning and late in the afternoon for babysitting purposes.** Teachers are even expected to call parents if their children aren't coming to school. It's my belief, however, **that the business of schools should simply be teaching.** We need to leave the socializing and babysitting of students to the parents.

WVIV: Dr. Stalley, we're about out of time. Maybe we can talk about this issue in more detail in a future broadcast.

COMPLEMENTATION

ADJECTIVE COMPLEMENTS

It	Linking Verb	Adjective	Noun Clause
It	seems	clear	**that society expects the schools to do everything.**

It	Linking Verb	Adjective of Urgency	Noun Clause with Base (Subjunctive) Form
It	is	essential	**that schools be smaller and that more teachers be hired.**

SUBJECT COMPLEMENTS

A main problem in education is **that the schools don't have a uniform curriculum.**

Grammar Notes

1. One type of noun clause functions as an adjective complement. It follows the pattern *It* + linking verb + adjective. (Some linking verbs are *be, seem, feel, smell, look, taste,* etc.). The clause further identifies or explains the adjective.

noun clause as adjective complement
It seems clear **that society expects the schools to do everything.**

This kind of sentence can be restated so that the noun clause becomes the subject of the sentence.

subject
That society expects the schools to do just about everything seems clear.

A sentence rearranged in this way is rarely heard in conversation.

2. When noun clauses in this pattern follow adjectives of urgency, the noun clause must contain the base (or subjunctive) form of the verb, since it is not known whether the action in the noun clause will ever take place. Expressions of urgency include *it is essential, it is necessary, it is important, it is advisable,* and *it is desirable.*

base form
It is essential that schools **be** smaller and
base form
that more teachers **be** hired. NOT ~~It is essential that schools are smaller and that more teachers are hired.~~

Sentences of this type can be restated, with the noun clause becoming the subject and occurring at the beginning of the sentence. Note that *it* is not needed in this restated sentence.

That more teachers be hired is essential.

A sentence arranged in this way is rarely heard in conversation.

3. Note that, as with sentences containing noun clauses after adjectives of urgency, certain verbs of urgency also require the base (or subjunctive) form of the verb in the noun clause. These verbs include *insist, demand, suggest,* and *recommend.*

The judge **insists** that Robert **be** at the hearing.

See Appendix 23 on page A26 for a list of verbs and expressions that require the base (or subjunctive) form of the verb in a following noun clause. See Unit 21 for more practice of this structure.

4. Another type of sentence contains a noun clause functioning as a subject complement.

The main problem in education is
noun clause functioning as subject complement
that the schools don't have a uniform curriculum.

In formal and academic writing this type of sentence often includes the words *the fact that* or *the belief that.*

The main problem in education is **the fact that the schools don't have a uniform curriculum.**

FOCUSED PRACTICE

1. Discover the Grammar

WVIV TV is covering a teachers' strike. Listen to the broadcast. Then listen again and underline the five noun clauses that function as adjective complements.

Reporter: We're stationed in front of the Board of Education building, where striking teachers are picketing and carrying signs, and it's obvious to even the most casual viewer that there are a lot of angry people here. Frances Baldwin, the spokesperson for the teachers' union, has agreed to talk with us. Ms. Baldwin, why are you all on strike?

Baldwin: Well, after three months of fruitless negotiations, it's clear that the Board of Education isn't taking our concerns seriously. It's important that the board do something positive if they want to break this impasse. Something has to change.

Reporter: What do you think has to happen?

Baldwin: It's absolutely essential that the board sincerely negotiate with us on our request for higher salaries, smaller classes, better discipline, and a real commitment to education.

Reporter: According to the president of the Board of Education, it's the students who are really going to come out the losers in this strike. What's your comment on that?

Baldwin: We sympathize with the students, and we want to get back to teaching them. However, we can't teach effectively now. The fact that there hasn't been a raise in teachers' salaries for six years shows the board's true colors. It's appalling that the board has refused even to talk with us. The students have just become pawns in this situation.

Reporter: All right, Ms. Baldwin. Thank you for your comments. Back to you in the studio, Ron.

2. What Do the Students Think?

KMBR went to a local high school and asked some students their opinion of their education. The results were mixed. Fill in the blanks in the conversation, using the indicated verbs and structures. Be sure to follow the sequence of tenses. Include the words **that** *and* **to** *in the appropriate places.*

Reporter: Thank you all for agreeing to talk with us. It's obvious that you are all concerned students.
1. (you / be / all / concerned students)
Rachel, let me start with you. How would you evaluate your education?

Rachel: It's lousy. I'd give it a poor grade.

Reporter: Why? What do you think is wrong with it?

Rachel: Well, it's pretty apparent ______________________. Most of them are just putting in their time and drawing a paycheck.
2. (a lot of the teachers / not / want / teach)

Reporter: Carlos, what do you think? Do you agree with Rachel?

Carlos: Not completely. It depends on the teacher. I've had some do-nothing types. But every once in a while you get a teacher who makes it clear ______________________ and ______________________.
3. (we / be / there / learn)
4. (he or she / be / there / teach)

(continued on next page)

Reporter: OK. Monique, what about you? What's been your experience?

Monique: I've had mostly good teachers.

Reporter: That's nice to hear. Who do you feel makes a good teacher?

Monique: For me it's someone who wants you to succeed. I had a fabulous math instructor last year who made it obvious from day one ______________________ but
5. (she / would / not tolerate / any nonsense)

______________________.
6. (she / be / there / help us / as much as / she / can)

Reporter: Uh-huh. OK, good. Andrew, where do you stand in this?

Andrew: I mostly agree with Rachel about the teachers. But it's also pretty clear

______________________.
7. (the whole system / need / be / change)

Reporter: What do you think needs to be done?

Andrew: Right now we study a lot of useless things. The Board of Education says everybody has to study English literature, but that's not important for me. I want to study automotive technology. Lots of times it's the students like me who lose out.

Reporter: Well, very interesting. I want to thank all of you for your excellent comments.

3. Demands

The Teachers' Union has written a list of demands that it wants to negotiate with the Board of Education. Write the union's demands in noun clauses in the form **it is** + adjective + clause.

1. It's necessary that class sizes be limited to twenty students.
(necessary / class sizes / be / limit / to twenty students)
____

2. ______________________
(essential / salaries / be / raise / at least 5 percent per year)
____

3. ______________________
(desirable / teachers / be / give / release time to complete special projects)
____

4. ______________________
(important / no instructor / be / ask / teach / more than five classes per day)
____

5. ______________________
(essential / strict discipline / be / maintain in the classroom)
____

4. Editing

For an English class assignment, a student has written a composition comparing two high school classes. Read the composition, and find and correct the nine errors.

Night and Day

Last year I took two classes, a history class and a Spanish class, that were as different as night and day. The history class was taught by Mr. Mattair, the basketball coach. From the start of the semester, it was obvious ~~what~~ *that* the class was going to be a total waste of time. Mr. Mattair made it clear right away that the basketball players going to be his special pets. Just about all we ever did was watch him diagram basketball plays on the chalkboard and listen to him tell stupid jokes. To pass the course, there were only two things that were necessary. One was that you were there every day to laugh at his jokes. The other was that you turned in a take-home midterm and final exam that you mostly copied out of the textbook. I didn't learn a bit of history the whole year. There was a TV interview with some students the other day, and a reporter asked this question: "What do you think needs to be changed to improve the educational system?" I'd say we need to get rid of teachers who can't and don't want to teach.

Mrs. Ochoa's Spanish class was 180 degrees away from Mr. Mattair's class. Starting on the first day, Mrs. Ochoa made it clear that we be there to learn Spanish. I can still remember what she told us: "If a student is going to learn Spanish, or any language, it's absolutely essential that he or she learns to speak it. We're going to be doing a lot of speaking in this class." Well, speak we did. We also read, wrote, listened to Spanish music, learned the geography of Spanish-speaking countries, and even taught our own mini-lessons. The class was hard, and at first some of the students didn't like the fact what Mrs. Ochoa kept us active for the whole fifty minutes every day. But by the end of the year, most of us could carry on a decent conversation in Spanish.

People say what the educational system is falling apart. The topic for this essay was "What do you think is necessary to improve the educational system?" The answer is "It needs more teachers like Mrs. Ochoa." The fact that teachers like Mrs. Ochoa be out there in the school system is evidence that our educational system isn't all bad.

COMMUNICATION PRACTICE

5. Practice Listening

Jim, a junior in high school, wants to drop out of school and get a job. He is talking with his cousin Frank, eight years older. Listen to the conversation. Then listen again and mark the following statements true (T) *or false* (F), *based on what you hear on the tape.*

__T__ 1. Jim believes that he doesn't belong in school.

_____ 2. Jim believes that he has learned something in school this year.

_____ 3. Jim believes that quitting school will make his life better.

_____ 4. Frank quit high school.

_____ 5. Frank's friends wanted to continue their friendship with him.

_____ 6. According to Jim, Frank's owning a house and a car is unimportant.

_____ 7. Frank thinks Jim should stick it out in school.

_____ 8. According to Frank, each individual has the chance to control the quality of his or her life.

_____ 9. Frank believes that the school system is definitely good.

_____ 10. According to Frank, each individual has the chance to control the quality of his or her education.

6. Role Play in Pairs

Work with a partner. Choose one of the following topics and role-play the situation. Then reverse the roles and play it again.

1. A student wants to get a better grade in a course and is talking with the teacher.

   Example:
   Student: I'm not doing as well in this course as I'd like to. What do you think would help me do better?
   Teacher: Well, it seems pretty apparent **that you're only interested in the grade you get.** I think it's important **that a student concentrate on learning the material.** The grades will follow naturally. That's what I'd suggest.

2. A student has been expelled from school for disciplinary reasons. The parents are discussing the problem with the school principal.
3. A principal has observed a teacher's class and has given the teacher a poor evaluation. The teacher disagrees. They are discussing the evaluation.
4. A student wants to drop out of school, but the parents don't agree. They are discussing the issue.

7. Debate

Choose one of the following topics to debate. Then divide into groups of six to eight. Three to four people should be on each side of the issue. Take time to prepare your argument.

Topic 1. Teachers should (OR should not) be paid on the basis of evaluations by their students.
Topic 2. Letter or numerical grades should (OR should not) be abolished as a means of evaluating students.
Topic 3. Starting with high school, a country's educational system should (OR should not) be structured so that students would choose between studying an academic or a vocational program.
Topic 4. School should (OR should not) be compulsory after the eighth year.

8. Letter

Write a letter to a politician (governor, premier, legislator, representative, etc.) about an educational reform that you think needs to be made. You may choose from the topics mentioned in the preceding debate or develop another topic. In your letter, state the problem that needs to be addressed, explain why you think it is a problem, offer possible solutions to the problem, and ask the politician to support your proposal legislatively.

9. Picture Discussion

This is an advertisement for life insurance. Why do you think the life insurance company presented this picture in its advertisement? Talk about the picture and speculate about the advertiser's intent.

Example:
It's obvious **that the father loves his child.**

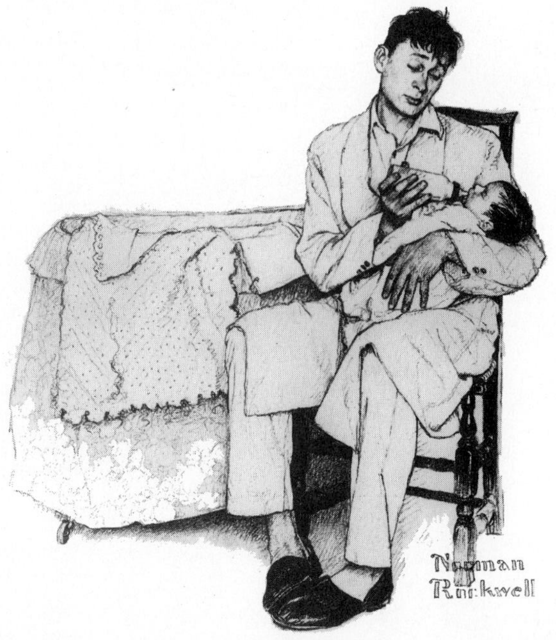

Norman Rockwell: (detail) Massachusetts Mutual "Father Feeding Infant." Photo courtesy of The Norman Rockwell Museum at Stockbridge.

PART VII

Review or SelfTest

I. *Read the conversations and underline each noun clause.*

1. **A:** I don't know what we should do tonight.

   B: Whatever you want to do is fine with me.

2. **A:** We haven't decided where we want to go on vacation.

   B: Don't you think that Hawaii would be nice?

3. **A:** How do we decide who wins the prize?

   B: Give the prize to whoever gets the most points.

4. **A:** Do you think she is guilty?

   B: Well, the fact that she waited so long to contact the police doesn't help her case.

5. **A:** I can't believe what I'm seeing. The Broncos might even win this game.

   B: Yeah, I know. I'm amazed that they've been able to do this well.

6. **A:** Mr. Jones, I'm sorry to say that I need more time to complete the assignment.

   B: That's all right. Take however long you need to do the job well.

7. **A:** In your view, what is the answer to the problem of violence in schools?

   B: I think that we need to ban weapons of all kinds.

8. **A:** What is Marilyn's problem?

   B: Well, it's clear that she's very unhappy.

II. *Read the letter, and find and correct the eight errors in pronouns that introduce noun clauses.*

November 28

Dear Manny,

Well, my first month as a literacy volunteer is over, and I feel exhilarated! ~~That~~ What I like best is the chance to work with real people. In the mornings I report to that's called "Open Classroom." I'm assigned to tutor whatever comes in and asks for help. Most of the students are wonderful; sometimes I'm amazed what they're so motivated to learn.

In the afternoons I tutor my regular students. I usually work with a lady from Vietnam named Mrs. Tranh. When I started working with her, she could hardly read at all, but I'm really impressed by who she's learned. At first I chose the assignments, but now we work on whoever Mrs. Tranh chooses. If she wants to practice reading aloud, that's that we do. If she wants to work on comprehension, we do that for whatever long she wants to do it. Sometimes we spend all afternoon on one thing, but it's very rewarding.

Well, that's all for now. Write soon, and I'll do the same.

Best,

Zeya

III. *Complete the conversations with noun clauses, using the words given. Be sure to include the word* **that** *if it is correct to do so.*

1. **A:** How long do you want to spend in San Francisco?

   B: However long you want to spend is fine with me.
   a. (However / long / you / want / spend)

2. **A:** Where's Hattie?

   B: I don't know ______________________. Maybe she's out in the back yard.
   b. (where / she / be)

3. **A:** Do you think ______________________?
   c. (Bill / be / an asset / to our firm)

   B: Well, ______________________ says something, I think.
   d. (the fact / he / ill / a great deal)

4. **A:** What do you think we need to do about Bill's excessive absences?

   B: I think ______________________ ______________________.
   e. (we / need / do) f. (whatever / be / necessary)

5. **A:** Who do you think is behind this rumor?

   B: I don't know, but ______________________ needs a talking to. It's obvious
   g. (whoever / it / be)
   ______________________. He has too much to lose.
   h. (it / not / be / Ron)

IV. *Read the sentences about education. Circle the letter of the correct answer to complete each sentence.*

1. ______________________ student test scores have not improved in the last decade suggests that the American educational system is in need of a major overhaul. A (B) C D
   - A. The fact which
   - B. The fact that
   - C. Which
   - D. What

2. Many educators seem convinced ______________________ students would respond favorably to a change in the system. A B C D
   - A. what
   - B. the fact
   - C. that
   - D. whatever

3. ______________________ America needs now is a two-track program in high schools. A B C D
   - A. Whatever
   - B. What
   - C. That
   - D. Whoever

4. In the majority of high schools at present, many students are allowed to take ________________ courses they want. A B C D
   A. whoever
   B. however
   C. whatever
   D. whenever

5. In a two-track system, students would choose after the eighth grade ________________ educational track they wanted to study: academic or vocational. A B C D
   A. which
   B. who
   C. whom
   D. when

6. ________________ was interested in a college education would study in the academic track. A B C D
   A. Whatever
   B. Whoever
   C. Whomever
   D. Whichever

7. ________________ wanted to go right into the workplace after graduation would choose the vocational track. A B C D
   A. Whoever
   B. However
   C. Whatever
   D. Whomever

8. ________________ America is one of only two industrialized nations without a two-track choice is a telling statistic. A B C D
   A. The fact which
   B. Which
   C. What
   D. That fact that

9. It is obvious ________________ the country needs this educational reform. A B C D
   A. what
   B. who
   C. which
   D. that

From Grammar to Writing

Writing Direct and Indirect Speech

1.

Direct speech quotes the exact words (or thoughts) of a speaker. Indirect speech (or reported speech) reports the words or thoughts of a speaker and contains most but not all of that speaker's exact words or thoughts.

Both direct and indirect speech usually occur in noun clauses, normally as direct objects.

direct speech
Jack asked Margo, **"Do you think James should go to a private school?"** (The quotation is the direct object of the verb, answering the question "What did Jack ask?")

indirect speech
Jack asked Margo **if she thought James should go to a private school.** (The noun clause **if she thought James should go to a private school** is the direct object, answering the question "What did Jack ask?")

2.

In direct speech, quotation marks surround the quotation. The reporting verb, such as *said, asked, told,* or *responded,* is followed by a comma if it introduces the quotation. Quotation marks come after a final period, question mark, or exclamation point.

James said**, "**Mom, I want to keep going to public school**."** (statement)
Margo asked Jack**, "**Can we afford to send James to a private school**?"** (question)
James said to Jack and Margo**, "**I won't go**!"** (exclamation)

If the reporting statement comes after the quotation, a comma follows the last word of the quotation, and the second set of quotation marks comes after the comma. A period ends the sentence.

"I don't want to go to a private school**,"** James said**.**

If the quotation is a question or an exclamation, that question or exclamation ends with a question mark or exclamation point.

"James, do you like school**?"** asked Aunt Colleen**.**
"I won't go to a private school**!"** James yelled.

If the reporting statement comes within the quotation, each part of the quotation is enclosed in quotation marks. The part of the quotation after the reporting statement does not begin with a capital letter if the remainder of the quotation is not part of a new sentence. Look at the quotation marks, the commas, and the capitalization in this example:

"Ms. Baldwin," **the reporter asked, "w**hy are you all on strike?"

3.

In indirect speech there are no quotation marks. The first word of the indirect speech is not capitalized. The reporting statement is not followed by a comma. An indirect question does not have a question mark at the end of the sentence. Note that indirect speech is presented as a noun clause and can be introduced by the word *that.*

James said **(that) he wanted to keep going to public school.**
James told his mom **(that) he wanted to keep going to public school.**
Margo asked Jack **if they could afford to send James to a private school.**

A. *Punctuate the following sentences in direct speech. Add capital letters if necessary.*

1. "Dad, I want to quit school and go to work," Jim murmured.
2. Sally, how would you evaluate your education the reporter queried
3. I absolutely despise going to school Sally responded (exclamation)
4. Jim, Frank said, you're crazy if you think it's going to be easy to get a job
5. Frank, said Jim, don't be a fool (exclamation)
6. The Teachers' Union spokesperson asked the superintendent when are you going to start taking our concerns seriously

B. *Correct the capitalization and punctuation in the following examples of indirect speech.*

1. Spokesperson Frances Baldwin said, that the Board of Education had even refused to talk to them.
2. Board President Bates responded that "There was simply no money for salary raises."
3. TV reporter Joan Matthews asked Fumiko if, she agreed with Sally that most teachers don't want to teach.
4. Frank asked Jim, What he would do if he couldn't find a job after he quit school?
5. Reporter Jim Bresler asked Zeya if she intended to go to college when her term was over

4.

In conversation and informal writing, the most common reporting verbs in both direct and indirect speech are *say, tell,* and *ask.* In more formal writing, the following reporting verbs are often used: *report, respond, query, wonder, confess, claim, maintain, add,* and *comment.*

Chairman Bates **maintained** that the school district had no money to raise teachers' salaries. (argued)
The teachers' union **claimed** that the chairman hadn't considered the union's demands. (expressed the opinion)

C. *In the following paragraph, change each instance of* **said** *to another reporting verb from the box.*

responded	maintained
claimed	added
commented	

Reporter Jennifer Goodenough asked Heidi Dennison what had been the single most enjoyable experience in her Peace Corps service. Heidi said (1. responded) that it had been the vacation she had taken to Kenya, Tanzania, and Uganda at the end of her first year. Jennifer said (2.) that she was surprised at Heidi's answer because she had expected her to mention one of her accomplishments in Nigeria. Many people said (3.) the purpose of the Peace Corps was to give Americans the chance to take vacations in exotic places. But Heidi said (4.) that the chance to learn about other countries was a valuable learning experience. She said (5.) that she thought it would contribute to international understanding in the long run.

PART VIII

Unreal Conditions

UNIT

20

Unreal Conditionals and Other Ways to Express Unreality

INTRODUCTION

Read and listen to the story and think about the questions.

Questions to Consider

1. Do you believe in intuition (knowing something without proof)?
2. Have you had any experiences in which your intuition or someone else's proved correct?

Intuition

It was a sweltering day. Thain and Aurora were driving down Maple Street, looking for a yard sale, when they spotted the old man. Waving at them with a halfhearted gesture, he looked **as if he hadn't eaten** for days.

"Honey, pull over. Let's give that old man a ride. He's going to faint if he doesn't get out of this sun."

"Thain, **I wish you'd stop** taking pity on every weirdo you see. He's probably an ax murderer. I bet he'll kill us and steal the car if we pick him up."

"I don't think so. He looks harmless to me—just a poor old guy. He's acting as if he's sick."

"But Sweetie, we have to get to that yard sale. There won't be anything worth buying if we don't get there soon."

"My male intuition is telling me we ought to stop."

"If I had a nickel for all the times we've done things because of your male intuition, I'd be a rich woman. Aren't females supposed to have the intuition, anyway? OK. I just hope we don't end up in the newspaper headlines. I can see it all now: YOUNG MARRIED COUPLE MUTILATED BY SERIAL KILLER!"

They pulled up to the curb in front of the old man. "Need some help, sir?" Thain asked.

The old man smiled. "Yes, thank you. Could you take me to a pharmacy? I'm diabetic and I've run out of medicine. I'm on a trip around the country, but I keep forgetting to buy enough insulin. If I don't take my medicine regularly, I go into shock. . . . **If only I weren't so forgetful.**"

They found a pharmacy and got the insulin. Back in the car, the old man said, "Now, if you can just take me to the bus station, I'll be on my way." Aurora frowned. Thain said, "Sure. We can do that." At the bus station, they helped the old man out of the car. "Can you tell me your names and your address? When I get back home, I'll send you a token of my appreciation." They gave him their names and address, said good-bye, and proceeded to the yard sale.

As Aurora had predicted, all of the good merchandise had been sold. **"I wish we'd been able to get here in time to buy that chest of drawers,"** she said, "but I'm glad we stopped for the old guy. He did need our help. I'll be surprised if we ever hear from him, though. You don't really believe all that about his taking a trip around the country, do you?"

In a few days they had forgotten about the incident. Three months later they returned from a short vacation, and Aurora was going through the pile of mail that had accumulated in their absence. She opened a long envelope with no return address.

"What in the world? Thain, come here and look at this!" There was a letter inside, neatly typed.

Dear Thain and Aurora,

I finished my trip around the country and had a marvelous time. I'm now back at home and shan't be traveling anymore, I don't think. I met some wonderful people in my travels, the two of you among them.

Thank you for your kindness to a forgetful old man. **If you hadn't come along when you did and taken me to the pharmacy, I might have died.** At the very least, **I would have become very ill. I wish that there had been time for us to get to know one another. If I had been fortunate to have any children of my own, I couldn't have had any nicer ones than you two.** At any rate, I am enclosing a token of my gratitude. My warmest regards,

Quentin Wilkerson

Something fluttered out of a second sheet of folded paper. It was a check for $50,000.

UNREAL CONDITIONALS AND OTHER WAYS TO EXPRESS UNREALITY

UNREAL CONDITIONALS

If I **had** a nickel for all the times we've done things because of your male intuition, I**'d be** a rich woman.
If you **hadn't helped** me, I **might have died.**
If my daughter **hadn't been given** poor advice, she would have taken the right courses.

OTHER WAYS TO EXPRESS UNREALITY

I **wish** (that) **I could** save money.
I **wish** (that) we**'d been able to get** to know one another better.
If only Barbara **would apply** herself.
If only I hadn't done that.
He acts **as though** he **were** president.
He acted **as if** he **hadn't eaten** for days.

Grammar Notes

1. Unreal Conditionals:

Conditional sentences consist of two clauses, a dependent *if*-clause and an independent result clause.

If-clause / result clause
If I had a car, I would drive to work.

Note the descriptions of unreality in the following examples.

a. In conditional sentences that express unreal ideas in the present time, use the simple past tense form of the verb in the *if*-clause and *would, could,* or *might* plus the base form of the verb in the result clause.

If I **were** you, I **would buy** a house. (Unreal: I'm not you.)

If we **had** enough money for a down payment, we **might buy** ten acres of land. (Unreal: We don't have enough money.)

If she **knew** Japanese well, she **could get** a job as an interpreter. (Unreal: She doesn't know Japanese very well.)

Be careful! Remember to use *were* for all persons with the verb *be*.

b. A variant form of the present unreal conditional is to use *were* plus an infinitive in the *if*-clause. The effect of this is to make the condition seem more tentative or hypothetical.

If I **were to offer** you a job, would you take it?

c. To express unreal ideas in the past time, use *had* plus a past participle in the *if*-clause, and use *would, could,* or *might* + *have* + past participle in the result clause.

If you **hadn't come along,** I **might have died.** (Unreal: You did come along.)

Usage note: You will hear some speakers use *would have* in the *if*-clause. However, this usage is not acceptable in formal speaking or writing.

If I **had known** he needed financial help, I would have lent him the money. NOT ~~If I **would have known** he needed financial help, I would have lent him the money.~~

2. Other Ways to Express Unreality:

a. Notice the difference between *wish* and *hope*. *Hope* is used to express a desire or an expectation about something that may be real or possible.

I **hope** he **comes** to the party. (And maybe he will.)
I **hope** he **wasn't** angry. (And maybe he wasn't.)

Wish is used to express a desire or a regret about something unreal and therefore not possible or probable. When talking about the present, use *wish* with a simple past tense verb or *would* or *could* plus a base form. Remember to use *were* for all persons of *be*.

I **wish** she **were** here now. (Unreal: She is not here now, and I regret that.)
I **wish** she **would work** faster. (Unreal: She is not willing to work faster.)

In past time, use *wish* with *had* + past participle.

I **wish** we **had been able to get** to know one another last year. (Unreal: We weren't able to get to know one another last year.)

b. The phrase *if only* has meanings somewhat similar to those of *wish* and *hope*. Use the simple past tense form after *if only* if you are wishing for something that is unreal at present.

If only she **loved** me. (Unreal: She doesn't love me.)

Use *had* plus a past participle after *if only* if you are wishing that something had happened differently in the past.

If only he **had buckled** his seat belt. (Unreal: He didn't buckle his seat belt.)

Use a simple present tense after *if only* if you are hoping for something that may become real in the present or future.

If only she **gets** the news on time!

c. Note the use of the phrases *as if* and *as though*. These forms are followed by simple present tense or *will* + base form to express situations that are probably real.

You are talking **as though** you **know** something about the crime. (Could be real)

d. *As if* and *as though* are often followed by past verb forms to express situations that are unreal or probably unreal. (Remember that in contrary-to-fact situations, *were* is used for all persons of *be*.) Note the sequence of tenses in the following examples:

He's acting **as if he were** the president. (Unreal: He's not the president.)
The old man looked **as though** he **hadn't eaten** for days. (Probably unreal)

Remember that when these are followed by simple present tense or *will* + base form, they express situations that could be real.

He's talking **as if** he**'ll be** president some day.

FOCUSED PRACTICE

1. Discover the Grammar

Read the following excerpt from a student's classroom speech on intuition. Underline clauses with real conditionals once and those with unreal conditionals twice.

How many of you believe in intuition? Is it just some sort of acting without thinking? If you act on the basis of intuition, will the results be disastrous? Today I'm going to try to convince you that intuition is more than some sort of mystical mumbo jumbo and that, if we all paid more attention to our intuitive feelings, we would do better.

Intuition is defined as a way of knowing something more or less immediately without having to go through a conscious process of figuring out the answer. In other words, if a new situation presents itself, you don't have to weigh the evidence on both sides of the question. You just know the answer.

Here's an example. You've been out of work for several months, so you apply for a job that will involve doing something you don't like. You get a call saying you've been selected for the job. Your intuition tells you that if you accept the job, you'll soon be bored and will hate it. Unfortunately, however, you suppress that idea and persuade yourself rationally that if you just approach the job with the right attitude, things will turn out well. Besides, you're desperate for employment, so you take the job and hope you end up liking it.

For a while you manage to act as if you liked the work, but you're only fooling yourself. Three months later you wish you hadn't been so hasty. You're miserable and hate going to work every day. "If only I'd waited a little longer," you say to yourself. If you'd listened to your intuition, you wouldn't be in this situation. By now you probably would have found a job more to your liking.

Where did you go wrong? You knew the answer to the question, but you ignored it. You didn't follow your intuition.

2. An Educational Trip

On the spur of the moment, Lee decided to visit the zoo. Later he wrote about the visit in his journal. Complete Lee's journal entry by writing unreal conditional forms after **as if** *or* **as though,** *using the verbs provided. Also complete the sentences containing* **I wish** *and* **I hope.**

August 28

Journal

Today I had the afternoon off. On the spur of the moment, I decided to visit the zoo. I hadn't been there in years, and I guess it might have been an angry letter-to-the-editor about zoo conditions that planted the idea in my head. My eyes were really opened.

The first thing I saw was the graffiti covering all the buildings near the entrance. The area almost looked as though it *had been abandoned* (1. be/abandon). I wish people ________ (2. have) more respect for public buildings. After all, we taxpayers are the ones who pay for them, ultimately. The next thing I noticed was that there was trash everywhere; the place looked as if it ________ (3. not/be/clean) for at least a month. I wish there ________ (4. be) more money to clean up the whole city, the zoo included.

Anyway, I kept walking and looked at all the animal exhibits, or should I say animal prisons. Aren't zoos supposed to be enlightened places these days? Not our zoo! Take the hippopotamus pond, for example. I could smell it from a hundred yards away. It's no wonder the pond stank; it appeared as though the water ________ (5. not/be/change) for months. Then I saw the monkeys in their cages. Poor creatures! They acted as if they ________ (6. give up) hope. Their cages were small and mostly filthy, and they just sat there in a dispirited manner.

I pushed on and saw the other animals in their exhibits, and their situations were all pretty much the same—especially the large animals like bears and cats. This sort of thing is so unfair to the animals. I hope someone ________ (7. do) something about this. At any rate, today was really a day of learning. I just wish I ________ (8. know) about this sooner. I'm going to write my senators.

3. Tragedy

Part 1 *Read and think about the poem. Then write past-time conditional sentences based on the verbs given. Use* **would** *unless another auxiliary, such as* **might** *or* **could,** *is given.*

'Out, Out—'
Robert Frost

The buzz saw snarled and rattled in the yard
And made dust and dropped stove-length sticks of wood,
Sweet-scented stuff when the breeze drew across it.
And from there those that lifted eyes could count
Five mountain ranges one behind the other
Under the sunset far into Vermont.
And the saw snarled and rattled, snarled and rattled,
As it ran light, or had to bear a load.
And nothing happened: day was all but done.
Call it a day, I wish they might have said
To please the boy by giving him the half hour
That a boy counts so much when saved from work.
His sister stood beside them in her apron
To tell them 'Supper.' At the word, the saw,
As if to prove saws knew what supper meant,
Leaped out at the boy's hand, or seemed to leap—
He must have given the hand. However it was,
Neither refused the meeting. But the hand!
The boy's first outcry was a rueful laugh,
As he swung toward them holding up the hand
Half in appeal, but half as if to keep
The life from spilling. Then the boy saw all—
Since he was old enough to know, big boy
Doing a man's work, though a child at heart—
He saw all spoiled. 'Don't let him cut my hand off—
The doctor, when he comes. Don't let him, sister!'
So. But the hand was gone already.
The doctor put him in the dark of ether.
He lay and puffed his lips out with his breath.
And then—the watcher at his pulse took fright.
No one believed. They listened at his heart.
Little—less—nothing!—and that ended it.
No more to build on there. And they, since they
Were not the one dead, turned to their affairs.

1. If the boy had been in school, he wouldn't have died.
(the boy / be / in school / he / not / die)

2. ______
(the doctor / arrive / sooner / he / might / be / able / save / the boy)

3. ______
(the boy / not / doing / a man's job / he / probably / not / be killed)

4. ______
(the saw / cut / the boy's finger instead of his hand / the boy / could probably / survive)

5. ______
(the boy / might / not / be cut by the saw / the sister / not say "supper" / at a crucial moment)

6. ______
(the work boss / say / "Call it a day" / the boy / escape / his fate)

Part 2 *Now assume that the time is the present and that the accident has just happened. Write sentences about what certain people probably wish or hope.*

7. The sister probably wishes (that) everyone had decided to quit work early.
(The sister / probably / wish / everyone / decide / quit work early)

8. ______
(The doctor / probably wish / he / arrive sooner)

9. ______
(The boy's parents / probably wish / they / not allow / the boy / work at a man's job)

10. ______
(Other parents / probably hope / this kind of accident / not happen / to their children)

4. Editing

Read the following diary entry. Find and correct the ten errors in conditionals.

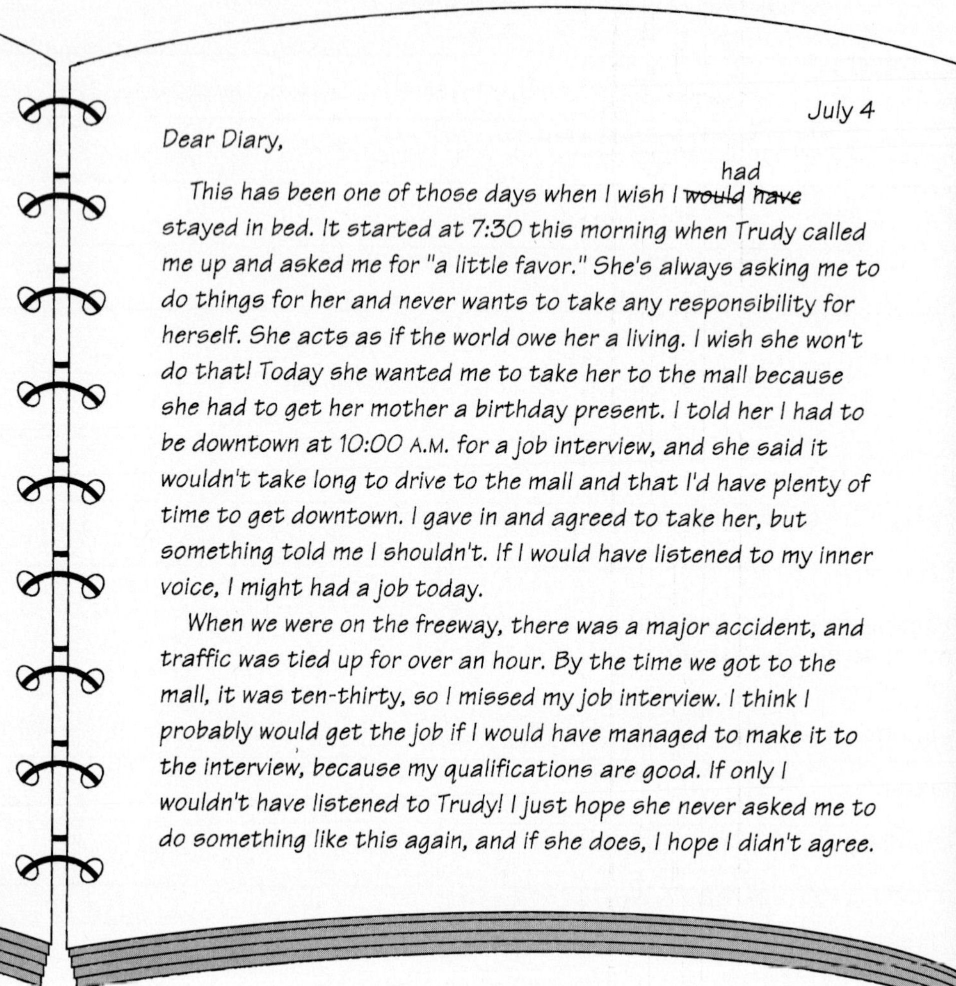

July 4

Dear Diary,

This has been one of those days when I wish I ~~would have~~ had stayed in bed. It started at 7:30 this morning when Trudy called me up and asked me for "a little favor." She's always asking me to do things for her and never wants to take any responsibility for herself. She acts as if the world owe her a living. I wish she won't do that! Today she wanted me to take her to the mall because she had to get her mother a birthday present. I told her I had to be downtown at 10:00 A.M. for a job interview, and she said it wouldn't take long to drive to the mall and that I'd have plenty of time to get downtown. I gave in and agreed to take her, but something told me I shouldn't. If I would have listened to my inner voice, I might had a job today.

When we were on the freeway, there was a major accident, and traffic was tied up for over an hour. By the time we got to the mall, it was ten-thirty, so I missed my job interview. I think I probably would get the job if I would have managed to make it to the interview, because my qualifications are good. If only I wouldn't have listened to Trudy! I just hope she never asked me to do something like this again, and if she does, I hope I didn't agree.

COMMUNICATION PRACTICE

5. Practice Listening

Listen to the conversation between two women who are members of Warm Hearts, a matchmaking service. Then listen again. For each item given, circle the letter of the sentence that explains the meaning of certain of the sentences you hear.

1. (a.) Rosa has met some interesting people.
   b. Rosa hasn't met any interesting people.
2. a. Phyllis followed her intuition.
   b. Phyllis didn't follow her intuition.
3. a. Phyllis went out with Les.
   b. Phyllis went out with Wayne.
4. a. Phyllis didn't pay attention to her feelings.
   b. Phyllis did pay attention to her feelings.
5. a. Phyllis is in a good relationship now.
   b. Phyllis isn't in a good relationship now.
6. a. Wayne seemed to think he was Phyllis's boss.
   b. Wayne didn't seem to think he was Phyllis's boss.
7. a. Phyllis thinks it's possible or likely that Wayne is gone for good.
   b. Phyllis thinks it's unlikely or improbable that Wayne is gone for good.
8. a. Phyllis doesn't regard herself as a coward.
   b. Phyllis regards herself as a coward.
9. a. Rosa thinks Phyllis puts herself down too much.
   b. Rosa doesn't think Phyllis puts herself down too much.
10. a. Phyllis thinks it's possible that Les hasn't found someone else.
    b. Phyllis thinks that Les has probably found someone else.

6. Discussion in Pairs

Work with a partner. Interview your partner about something in the past he or she wishes had turned out differently. Then reverse the roles.

7. Essay

Write an essay of three to five paragraphs about a time when you ignored your intuition and inner "gut" feelings and opted instead for a rational decision which turned out unsuccessfully. Describe your original intuitive feeling, explain why you ignored it, and speculate on what would or might have happened if you had acted intuitively.

8. Picture Discussion

Look at this picture. Discuss the events that may have led to this situation. Then divide into two groups. One group will explore the woman's point of view while the other group will speculate on Brad's point of view. Finally, talk as a class about what Brad and the woman might wish.

Roy Lichtenstein, *Drowning Girl.* (1963)
Oil and synthetic polymer paint on canvas, 67 5/8 x 66 3/4".
The Museum of Modern Art, New York. Philip Johnson Fund and gift of Mr. and Mrs. Bagley Wright.

UNIT

21

Inverted and Implied Conditionals; Subjunctive in Noun Clauses

INTRODUCTION

Read and listen to the letter to the advice columnist and the columnist's response.

Questions to Consider

1. In your opinion, what is the difference between being assertive and being aggressive?
2. Do you agree with the saying "Don't say yes when you mean no"?

Dear Pamela,
I've always been considered a "nice guy," but I guess you could also call me "a soft touch." A year ago my wife's brother, Stan, was in a desperate situation and needed a thousand dollars immediately to pay off a loan he had defaulted on. He **asked that we lend him the money.** At first I **suggested that he go through the usual channels and get a bank loan.** He said he'd tried that and had been turned down. He pressured my wife for a loan, and she pressured me. He assured us that if we lent him the money, he would pay it back with interest. I gave in and advanced him a thousand dollars from my own account, but I shouldn't have. In fact, **had I known what was going to happen, I never would have said yes.** We didn't put anything in writing, and Stan hasn't paid us a cent. I am extremely angry about this, but whenever I mention it to Carol, my wife, she says that Stan is going through a rough time right now, and **it's important that we keep peace in the family.** Pamela, what should I do?

Furious in Frankfort

Dear Furious,
Sweetie, it's one thing to be a nice guy, but it's another to be a doormat. It sounds like you let people take advantage of you. **If so,** I'd say it's time you got some assertiveness training; **without it,** you'll just keep letting people tell you what to do.

In my view you should have **insisted that Stan sign** a notarized agreement spelling out the terms of repayment. It's too late for that now, though, so I **recommend that you arrange** a meeting between yourself and Stan. Leave Carol out of it. Perhaps you can call and ask Stan to meet you for lunch at a restaurant. At the lunch meeting, tell him calmly but in no uncertain terms that you're angry and that this thing has gone far enough. **Insist that he start** making immediate repayments. **Should he balk** at what you're saying or mention Carol, simply tell him that this is between you and him, that you don't want family squabbles, and that there won't be any as long as he makes the payments. Make it clear that he *must* make the payments; **if not,** you'll take him to small claims court. **It's essential that Stan understand** that you're serious; **otherwise,** he'll simply go on taking advantage of you.

Tell Carol what you've done after you've met with Stan. You don't need to get angry; just say that it was your money that was lent, that this is the way things are going to be from now on, and that you'd rather you and she not get into a fight about it.

Then look around for a course in assertiveness. **With a little work,** you can learn not to let people walk all over you. Good luck, and be calm but courageous!

Pamela

Inverted and Implied Conditionals; Subjunctive in Noun Clauses

INVERSION

Had I known what would happen, I wouldn't have advanced him the money.
Were she to apologize now, I would forgive her.
Should you return before I do, please pick up the mail.

IMPLIED CONDITIONALS

I don't believe you want to get a divorce. **If so,** you would have already left.
Without your help, I would never have been able to get there on time.
What if I offered you this job?

SUBJUNCTIVE IN NOUN CLAUSES FOLLOWING CERTAIN VERBS AND ADJECTIVES

I insist (that) she **be** here by the time the session begins.
It is important that you **be** aware of certain facts.
It is essential that he **start** accepting responsibility.

Grammar Notes

1. You can express an unreal condition by deleting *if* and inverting the auxiliaries *had, were,* or *should* and the subject in an *if*-clause.

   Had I known that would happen, I wouldn't have advanced him the money. (= If I had known . . .)
   Were I to offer you a job, I'd need a strong recommendation from your former employer. (= If I were to offer you a job . . .)
   Should that happen, I'd be ready for it. (= If that should happen . . .)

2. Unreal and real conditionals are sometimes implied rather than stated directly with an *if*-clause and a result clause. Implied conditionals often use the following phrases and words: *if so, if not, otherwise, with,* and *without.*

   Without a clear policy, you would continue to be manipulated by others. (**Without** = If you didn't have . . .)
   With some training, you could learn not to be a doormat. (**With** = If you got . . .)
   It sounds like you let people take advantage of you. **If so**, you need to learn to be more assertive. (**If so** = if you do let people take advantage of you . . .)
   If not, maybe you're just unlucky. (**If not** = If you don't let people take advantage of you . . .)
   Stan needs to understand that you're serious. **Otherwise,** he'll continue taking advantage. (**Otherwise** = If he doesn't understand . . .)
   What if I told you the truth? (= What would happen if I told you the truth?)

3. The subjunctive form of the verb is used in a noun clause following adjectives and verbs of urgency. The subjunctive form is used to convey a sense of unreality of the outcome at the moment the statement is made. It is impossible to know whether the action in the noun clause will ever occur.

   It is essential that he **understand** clearly what you want. (It may be essential, but we don't know if he will or he won't.)
   I suggest that she **go** to the doctor first thing in the morning. (I may suggest it, but I can't know if she will actually go.)

4. Two commonly used expressions, *it's time* and *would rather,* are followed by the base form (subjunctive) or the simple past tense form of the verb.

   They'd rather we **didn't smoke** here.
   I'd rather she **use** only English in class.
   It's time you **grew** up!

FOCUSED PRACTICE

1. Discover the Grammar

Read and listen to the following radio advertisement on assertiveness training. Then underline all subjunctive verb forms and circle all implied conditionals.

A few minutes ago your friend Mary called and asked that you babysit her children for the fifth time in the last three weeks. Had you known she was going to call, you wouldn't have answered the phone. The last time this happened, it was ten o'clock at night and Mary still hadn't picked up her kids. You finally had to call and insist that she come and get them. You politely suggested that Mary look into day care, but she said she wouldn't be able to afford it until she got a job. After that you swore you wouldn't be manipulated again, but when Mary called up and said, "Just this once," you gave in and said yes. Now you're boiling inside, though, because you feel Mary treats you like her slave.

Does this sound like you? If so, we can help. We're Lionhearts, and we specialize in assertiveness training. With a little bit of practice, you can learn how to say what you think and not feel guilty about it. Call 232-9195 now for an appointment. Money back if you're not completely satisfied.

2. Growing Up

Complete the sentences with past forms of the indicated verbs after **what if, would rather, as if,** *and* **it's time.**

Dad: Liz, the swim meet starts in an hour. It's time we ___were leaving___ (1. be leaving).

Liz: Dad, can't I just go by myself? I'd rather you and Mom ________ (2. let) me drive. I do have my license, you know.

Dad: Liz, it's a dangerous world out there. What if you ________ (3. get) into an accident?

Liz: Dad, I'm sixteen years old. It's time you and Mom ________ (4. start) treating me like an adult.

Dad: You're not an adult yet, Liz.

Liz: OK, maybe not, but you guys treat me as if I ________ (5. be) a baby. It's embarrassing, always getting dropped off.

Dad: Hmm. All right. Do you really think you can handle it?

Liz: Of course, Dad.

3. Aggressiveness vs. Assertiveness

Complete the following page from The Assertive Individual's Handbook. *Use subjunctive forms of the indicated verbs in the noun clauses. Read the page from left to right, following the numbered items in order.*

The Agressive Person	The Assertive Person
1. The aggressive person insists that *she be allowed* (she/be/allow) to have her own way.	2. The assertive person requests that ______ (her way/be/consider).
3. For an aggressive person, it is essential that ______ (an argument/be/win).	4. For an assertive person, it is important that ______ (an argument/be) fair.
5. The aggressive person demands that ______ (you/adopt) his viewpoint.	6. The assertive person asks that ______ (you/give) consideration to his viewpoint.
7. An aggressive person is likely to order that ______ (something/be/do).	8. An assertive person is likely to suggest that ______ (a course of action/be/follow).

4. Job Hunting

Fill in the blanks in the story with items from the box.

if so	if not	with	otherwise	had she stayed	had she known

Linda had recently moved to Atlanta from Ponders, the small town where she had grown up. ___Had she known___ (1.) how difficult it would be to find employment, she might have stayed in her home town. She loved the big city, though, and she felt that, ________________ (2.) in Ponders, she would have fallen into a rut that she would never escape from. The only problem was that Linda needed to find a job soon; ________________ (3.), she wouldn't be able to pay next month's rent, and she'd have to go back to Ponders. The trouble was, she was shy about asking for work.

One day Linda was wandering around downtown, feeling that ________________ (4.) a bit of luck, she might find something. She saw a pleasant-looking florist's shop. Maybe they were hiring. ________________ (5.), she might get a job. ________________ (6.), she wouldn't lose anything by going in and asking. Without even thinking further, she walked in.

"I'm Linda Hilliard, and I was wondering whether you were doing any hiring. I have a lot of experience with flowers and gardening."

The manager said, "Actually, we do need someone to work part time. I was just going to put up a sign in the window. Tell me more about your experience."

Linda got the job.

Now rewrite the phrase in each blank above with an **if**-*clause that restates the meaning.*

7. ___If she had known___ (she / know)
8. ________________ (she / stay)
9. ________________ (she / not / find / work)
10. ________________ (she / have)
11. ________________ (they / be / hiring)
12. ________________ (they / not / be / hiring)

5. Editing

Read the letter. Find and correct the eight verb errors.

December 10

Dear April,

I wanted to write and fill you in on what's been happening since I left Ponders.

I finally got a job! Remember when you suggested I just ~~went~~ go walking around, getting a sense of what Atlanta was like? A few weeks ago I was really getting worried, and I had spent almost all the money I had saved up to tide me over until I found work. I had gotten to the point where it was absolutely essential that I found something or just came home. So I decided to try your advice. Had I know how easy this would be, I would have tried it the first week I was here. I started walking around in the downtown area, and before I knew it I saw a beautiful little florist's shop. I walked right in as if I have courage and experience and asked whether they had a job. Can you believe that they did?

I was really happy in my job until my boss hired a new assistant manager who has been making my life miserable. He treats me as if I be his personal slave. I took this job to work with plants, not to serve him coffee. I think it's time I'm telling him where I stand.

I have a few days off for the holidays. What if I had come home as a surprise to Mom and Dad? Could we plan some kind of party? Write and let me know, OK?

Love,

Linda

COMMUNICATION PRACTICE

6. Practice Listening

Listen to a segment of the radio talk show "Wimp No More."

Comprehension

Now listen again and mark the following statements true (T) *or false* (F), *based on what you hear.*

__T__ 1. Callers are supposed to turn down their radios when they're on the air.

_____ 2. Mildred's mother-in-law takes Buddy shopping every day.

_____ 3. Mildred's mother-in-law owns the house Mildred and Buddy live in.

_____ 4. Buddy's mother treats Mildred like an intruder.

_____ 5. Buddy doesn't want his mother to set foot in the house.

_____ 6. Buddy doesn't want Mildred to excite his mother.

_____ 7. Forrest thinks Mildred needs to do something about the situation soon.

_____ 8. Forrest will sit down with Buddy and tell him the situation can't continue.

_____ 9. Forrest thinks Buddy should find his mother a new place to live.

_____ 10. Buddy got mad and chose his mother over Mildred.

_____ 11. Forrest suggests that Buddy take a chance and get married.

Optional Dictation

Now listen once more, filling in the blanks in certain of the sentences.

1. We ____ask____ only ____that you turn down____ your radio when you're on the air
2. and __________ your language clean.
3. She __________ her shopping every day
4. and __________ dinner with her.
5. She makes it seem __________ the place
6. and I __________ some sort of intruder.
7. I __________ set foot in the house.
8. He says it's really __________ her too much.
9. __________ some action here.
10. If __________ with Buddy and tell him this can't go on.

11. I ______________________________ her a new place to live.
12. ______________________________ get mad and choose her over me?
13. I ______________________________ Buddy a chance to show who he's married to.

7. Role Play in Pairs

Work with a partner. Choose one of the following situations and role-play it. Then reverse the roles and play it again.

1. A spouse who feels under the control of an in-law has decided to confront the in-law about the problem.
2. A parent and a strong-willed child are having an argument. The parent is having difficulty with the child, who is refusing to do chores.
3. Two spouses are having a discussion. One spouse feels constantly belittled and put down by the other but has decided to confront the other spouse about the problem.

8. Essay

Choose one of the following topics and write a narrative essay of three or four paragraphs about it.

Topic 1. A time when being assertive was a mistake for you. What happened? What should you have done instead? What might have happened had you behaved differently?

Topic 2. A time when you weren't assertive and should have been. What did you do? What could you have done?

Topic 3. A time when you were successfully assertive. What action did you take? Why was it successful?

9. Picture Discussion

In groups of four or five, discuss this picture. Talk about what you think the artist might have wanted to show. What do you think the title means? Then discuss your group's ideas and opinions with those of the other groups.

Example:
The artist seems to treat time **as if it were** . . .

Salvador Dalí, *Persistence of Memory.* (1931)
Oil on canvas, 9 1/2 x 13".
The Museum of Modern Art. Given anonymously.
Photograph ©1995 The Museum of Modern Art, New York.

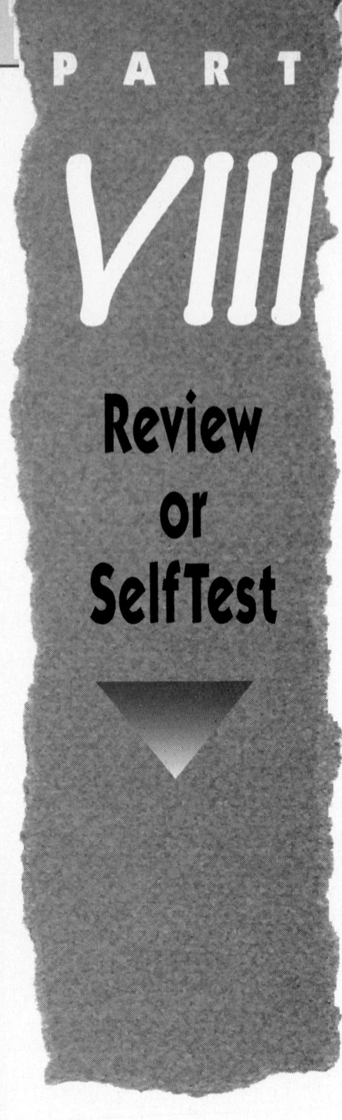

I. *Read the paragraph about Brandon's car problem. Then complete the sentences with conditional forms.*

Recently I had an experience that taught me a lesson. I'd been meaning to get the oil in my car changed, but I kept putting it off. Last Tuesday on the Appleton Expressway I was on my way to a job interview when the car just quit. The engine seized because it was out of oil. Before I could make it to the side of the road, another car rear-ended me. That did about a thousand dollars worth of damage to the car, and I had to have the car's engine completely replaced. I had to pay a towing bill of $150, and I didn't make it to the job interview, either. Hopefully, I've learned my lesson.

1. Brandon wishes he hadn't put off changing the oil in the car.
(Brandon / wish / not put off / changing the oil in the car)
____
2. _______________
(If / he / change / the oil / the engine / not seize)
____
3. _______________
(If / the engine / not seize / the other car / not rear-end him)
____
4. _______________
(He / not / have to / pay a towing bill)
____
5. _______________
(He / not / have to / replace the engine)
____
6. _______________
(He / could / make it to the job interview / if / all this / not happen)
____
7. _______________
(If / he / make it to the job interview / he might / get the job)
____
8. _______________
(Brandon / hope / that / he / learn his lesson)
____

II. *Complete the conversations with* **as if/as though** *and the correct form of the verb.*

1. **A:** Harriet is really arrogant, don't you think?

B: Yes. She's always acting as if she were the boss.
(as if / she / be)

2. **A:** How's the weather there?

B: Well, an hour ago it looked _______________ pour.
(as though / it / going to)
The sun is shining now, though.

3. **A:** Chief, Mr. Bransford is acting ______________________ guilty.
(as if / he / be)

B: Just remember, Officer, that he's innocent until proven guilty.

4. **A:** Where did you get this dog? He's really cute.

B: We found him on the street. He looked ______________________ in some sort of accident.
(as though / he / be)
He's OK now, though.

5. **A:** What do you think of our new boss?

B: She needs to be more decisive. She's acting ______________________ one of the
(as if / she / be)
employees.

6. **A:** What are you so mad about?

B: You're behaving ______________________ this whole thing was my fault. I didn't have
(as though / you / think)
anything to do with it, remember?

III. *Read the answer from an advice columnist. Then complete five subjunctive sentences that restate the columnist's suggestions.*

To Mary in Montreal:

No one should have to put up with a dog that barks all night. First, it's essential for you to talk with your next-door neighbor. At the same time, though, it's important not to lose your temper while you're explaining your side of the issue. Ask your neighbor to bring the dog in at night. Stay calm. If she refuses to, insist on her getting rid of the animal. If all else fails, I'd recommend calling the animal control bureau.

1. It is essential that Mary
talk with her next-door neighbor.

2. It is important that Mary
____
while she is explaining her side of the issue.

3. Mary should ask that her neighbor
______________________.

4. If she refuses to, Mary should insist that she
______________________.

5. The columnist recommends that Mary
____
if all else fails.

IV. *Complete the conversation by writing verb phrases with* **wish, hope,** *and* **if only.**

Aurora: I can't believe Mr. Wilkerson sent us a check for $50,000. I wish ___we'd been able to___ (1. we / be able to) get better acquainted with him the day he was here.

Thain: Yeah. If only ______________ (2. we / realize) what was happening.

Aurora: I just hope ______________ (3. he / keep) taking his insulin, and I hope ______________ (4. there / be) someone around to remind him in case he forgets.

Thain: You know, I really wish ______________ (5. we can / contact) him in some way. The trouble is, there's no return address on the envelope. Hey! What about the postmark? Where is that envelope, anyway?

Aurora: Here it is. Oh, no. Look at this! If only the postmark ______________ (6. not / be) so blurred. You can't see the city name.

Thain: I wish ______________ (7. we / have) a magnifying glass. . . . Hey, wait; I can make out the zip code. It's 93302. Honey, get the almanac, will you?

Aurora: Here it is. Zip codes that start with nine are on the West Coast, aren't they? I hope ______________ (8. this / not / be) like finding a needle in a haystack. Try California.

Thain: OK. . . . Here it is! 93302—that's Bakersfield. I wish ______________ (9. we / know) someone in Bakersfield.

Aurora: I know! Let's go to the library and look in the Bakersfield telephone directory. Maybe his name will be listed. Let's hope ______________ (10. it / be).

V. *Circle the letter of the correct answer to complete each sentence.*

1. You need to get some job retraining. ______________ it, you risk being laid off.   A   B   C   (D)
   A. If so
   B. If not
   C. With
   D. Without

2. I recommend that Miriam ______________ a boarding school. She'd be much more challenged academically.   A   B   C   D
   A. attends
   B. attend
   C. is attending
   D. were attending

3. Ambrose had to take a job at a fast-food restaurant; ______________, he wouldn't have been able to make his car payment.   A   B   C   D
   A. otherwise
   B. if so
   C. had he done so
   D. were that the case

4. I hope you ______________________ make it to the family reunion on the fifteenth. Everyone will be there. A B C D
   A. could
   B. were
   C. can
   D. should

5. I hope Anna passed her exams. ______________________, she'll have to repeat her senior year. A B C D
   A. If not
   B. Without
   C. With
   D. If so

6. At this point, Shannon wishes she ______________________ mechanical drawing. She hates the course. A B C D
   A. didn't take
   B. wouldn't take
   C. hadn't taken
   D. were to take

7. You were right when you suggested I ______________________ my intuition in this business deal. I did, and it worked. A B C D
   A. follow
   B. followed
   C. were to follow
   D. had followed

8. I wish we ______________________ to get to know one another better in the time we had. A B C D
   A. will be able
   B. were able
   C. would have been able
   D. had been able

9. I'll be home by 7:00 P.M. on the eighteenth. ______________________ before me, please pick up the mail. A B C D
   A. Should arrive
   B. Should you arrive
   C. You should arrive
   D. Should you have arrived

10. It sounds like something is wrong with the car's engine. ______________________, we'd better take it to the garage immediately. A B C D
   A. Otherwise
   B. Without it
   C. If not
   D. If so

From Grammar to Writing

Avoiding Run-on Sentences and Comma Splices

1.

A sentence is made up of at least one independent clause. A sentence containing more than one independent clause must be punctuated properly to avoid two kinds of errors: the run-on sentence and the comma splice.

<u>A run-on sentence</u> is a group of words containing at least two independent clauses without any punctuation separating them; the sentences are "run together."

independent clause — independent clause

> Thain and Aurora were on their way to a yard sale an old man waved feebly to them.

The following are four ways to correct a run-on sentence.

a. Separate the two independent clauses with a period. Capitalize the first word of the second clause.

> Thain and Aurora were on their way to a yard sale**. A**n old man waved feebly to them.

b. Separate the two independent clauses with a semicolon. Do not capitalize the first word of the second clause.

> Thain and Aurora were on their way to a yard sale**; a**n old man waved feebly to them.

c. Join the two independent clauses with a comma and a coordinating conjunction.

> Thain and Aurora were on their way to a yard sale**, and** an old man waved feebly to them.

d. Make one of the independent clauses dependent by adding a subordinating conjunction, and separate the two clauses with a comma if the dependent clause comes first.

> **When** Thain and Aurora were on their way to a yard sale**,** an old man waved feebly to them.

A. *Correct the following run-on sentences by using the method suggested.*

1. The old man had forgotten to buy medicine he went into diabetic shock. (period)
2. Thain asked Aurora to pull over his intuition told him the old man needed their help. (semicolon)
3. Kate knew she had to change her relationship with her boss she didn't know how to do it. (coordinating conjunction and comma)
4. Aurora wished they had gotten to the yard sale on time she was glad they had stopped to help the old man. (subordinating conjunction at beginning of sentence and comma)

2.

A comma splice is the joining of two independent clauses with only a comma. A comma, however, does not provide adequate separation.

independent clause independent clause

Marsha read *The Assertive Individual's Handbook,* she learned a lot about expressing herself in the process.

A comma splice can be corrected by the same four methods used to correct a run-on sentence.

a. Use a period.

Marsha read *The Assertive Individual's Handbook*. **S**he learned a lot about expressing herself in the process.

b. Use a semicolon.

Marsha read *The Assertive Individual's Handbook*; **s**he learned a lot about expressing herself in the process.

c. Use a comma and a coordinating conjunction.

Marsha read *The Assertive Individual's Handbook*, **and** she learned a lot about expressing herself in the process.

d. Make one of the clauses dependent by adding a subordinating conjunction.

When Marsha read *The Assertive Individual's Handbook*, she learned a lot about expressing herself in the process.

A fifth way of correcting a comma splice is to convert one of the clauses into an adverbial *-ing* phrase if the subjects of the two clauses are the same.

Marsha read *The Assertive Individual's Handbook*, **learning a lot about herself in the process.**

The period and semicolon are similar punctuation marks in that they are both used between independent clauses. The period can be thought of as separating two clauses and the semicolon as joining two clauses.

Do not capitalize the first word after a semicolon (unless it is *I* or a proper noun).

The teachers considered the Board of Education's offer; **t**hen they went on strike.

Use a semicolon instead of a period to join independent clauses if you feel that the two clauses have a close connection in meaning.

Kate's job situation deteriorated a great deal; **s**he had to speak to her boss.

Be careful! Do not use a semicolon to connect an independent clause and a dependent clause.

While I was learning to be assertive, **I** learned many things about myself.

NOT

~~While I was learning to be assertive; I learned many things about myself.~~

B. *Correct each of the following comma splices by using the suggested method in each case.*

1. The old man looked ill, he needed to get out of the sun quickly. (semicolon)
2. Thain and Aurora drove to a pharmacy, they got the old man his insulin. (period)
3. Aurora wanted to get to the yard sale, there was a chest of drawers for sale. (semicolon)
4. Aurora didn't want to stop for the old man, Thain persuaded her it was necessary. (comma and coordinating conjunction)
5. Harold says he will seek professional help to overcome his anger, there is no assurance that he will carry out his promise. (subordinating conjunction at beginning of sentence, dependent clause and comma)
6. Nancy felt dominated by her mother-in-law, she needed to take assertive action. (Convert the first clause to an adverbial *-ing* phrase and place the noun subject in the second clause.)

3.

Notice the specific types of punctuation in sentences containing transitions.

> You are three months behind in paying your electric bill; therefore, we are terminating your service.
>
> You need to take some positive action. Also, you need to respect yourself.

If a transition begins a clause, place a period or a semicolon before it. Remember to use a semicolon if you feel that the clauses connected are closely related in meaning; otherwise, use a period.

C. *Correct the following run-on sentences, using the suggested punctuation mark in each case. Capitalize where necessary.*

1. A tiny voice inside Arthur told him he would hate the job;‸ therefore, he turned it down. (semicolon)
2. Nancy says she wants to do something worthwhile if so, she should join the Peace Corps. (period)
3. I need to get a bank loan otherwise, I'll have to file for bankruptcy. (semicolon)
4. Jack and Margo would like to send James to a private school however, the school is expensive, and James doesn't want to go. (period)
5. Becky and David love their new neighborhood in fact, they're going to buy a house there. (semicolon)

D. *Carefully read and study the following passage, which contains thirteen independent clauses. Correct the errors in run-on sentences and comma splices by adding periods or semicolons and capitalizing correctly.*

Call it either intuition or good vibrations. Whatever you want to call it, it works last summer, I was one of four members of a committee to hire a new head nurse at the nursing home where I work we interviewed two candidates as finalists, a man named Bob and a woman named Sarah on paper, Bob was better qualified he had had extensive experience in a similar position, while Sarah had only had one administrative job however, Sarah was the one who really impressed us she answered all of the questions straightforwardly and simply Bob, on the other hand, evaded some of our questions while simultaneously trying to make us think he knew everything and could do everything all of us on the committee simply liked Sarah better in fact, she got the job because she was the person we all felt we wanted to work with. Our intuition wasn't wrong she's turned out to be a wonderful head nurse.

Appendices

1. Verb Tense Charts

SIMPLE PRESENT

USES
For habitual actions: She **eats** cereal for breakfast.
For general truths or general present: Water **boils** at 100°C.
For a definite and close future: The course **starts** tomorrow afternoon.

FORM	
AFFIRMATIVE	
Base form	They **eat** cereal for breakfast.
Third-person singular form	She **eats** cereal for breakfast.
NEGATIVE	
Do + *not* + base form	They **don't eat** cereal for breakfast.
Does + *not* + base form	She **does not eat** cereal for breakfast.

SIMPLE PAST

USES
For completed past actions: We **saw** *Citizen Kane* last night.
For habitual past actions: We **saw** a movie every Saturday.

FORMS	
AFFIRMATIVE	
Regular verb: base form + *-ed*	We **liked** *Citizen Kane.*
Irregular verb: see Appendix 2	We **ate** dinner before the show.
NEGATIVE	
Did + *not* + base form	We **didn't like** the movie theater.
	We **didn't eat** afterwards.

FUTURE

USES
For future actions or plans: They **will call** next Monday.
For promises (with *will*): I **will** always **be** there for you.

FORMS	
AFFIRMATIVE	
Will + base form	He **will call** tomorrow.
Am/is/are going to + base form	He**'s going to call** tomorrow.
NEGATIVE	
Will + *not* + base form	He **will not call** today.
Won't + base form	He **won't call** tonight.
Am/is/are + *not going to* + base form	He **is not going to call** on Tuesday.

PRESENT PROGRESSIVE

USES
For present actions: They **are talking** on the phone.
For a close future: We **are going** in five minutes.

FORMS	
AFFIRMATIVE	
Am + progressive form	I **am writing** a letter.
Is + progressive form	She **is sleeping**.
Are + progressive form	They **are listening** to music.
NEGATIVE	
Am + *not* + progressive form	I **am not writing** a letter.
Is + *not* + progressive form	She **is not sleeping**.
Are + *not* + progressive form	They **are not listening** to music.

PAST PROGRESSIVE

USES
For actions in progress in the past: Matthew **was skiing** when he broke his ankle.

FORMS	
AFFIRMATIVE	
Was/were + progressive form	I **was talking** to Isao. They **were playing** the guitar last night.
NEGATIVE	
Was/were + *not* + progressive form	I **wasn't talking** to Isao. They **were not playing** the guitar last night.

FUTURE PROGRESSIVE

USES
For an action in progress in the future: She **will be traveling** in Spain next fall.

FORMS	
AFFIRMATIVE	
Will + *be* + progressive form	We **will be talking** to Dr. Tanaka tomorrow.
NEGATIVE	
Will + *not* + *be* + progressive form	We **will not be talking** to Dr. Tanaka tomorrow.
Won't + *be* + progressive form	We **won't be talking** to Dr. Tanaka tomorrow.

PRESENT PERFECT

USES
For an action that began in the past and continues: I **have wanted** that bike for months. For something that has been experienced: I **have taken** the train many times.

FORMS	
AFFIRMATIVE	
Have + past participle	I **have studied** marine biology for two years.
Has + past participle	She **has studied** marine biology for two years.
NEGATIVE	
Have + *not* + past participle	I **have not worked** here for very long.
Has + *not* + past participle	He **has not worked** here for very long.

PAST PERFECT

USES
For an action that was completed in the past before another past action: I **had seen** that movie many times before I began to understand it.

FORMS	
AFFIRMATIVE	
Had + past participle	She was tired because she **had run** in the race.
NEGATIVE	
Had + *not* + past participle	She **had not competed** before.

FUTURE PERFECT

USES
For an action that will be completed before another future action: By the year 2000, scientists **will have made** many new discoveries.

FORMS	
AFFIRMATIVE	
Will + *have* + past participle	We **will have found** new sources of energy.
NEGATIVE	
Will + *not* + *have* + past participle	By 11:00, we **will not have finished** the exam.
Won't + *have* + past participle	By 11:00, we **won't have finished** the exam.

PRESENT PERFECT PROGRESSIVE

USES
For an action that began in the past and continues: I **have been waiting** for hours.

FORMS	
AFFIRMATIVE	
Have + *been* + progressive form	Environmentalists **have been trying** to save the spotted owl.
Has + *been* + progressive form	Sally Trezona **has been trying** to save the spotted owl.
NEGATIVE	
Have + *not* + *been* + progressive form	I **have not been working** very hard.
Has + *not* + *been* + progressive form	He **has not been working** very hard.

PAST PERFECT PROGRESSIVE

USES
For a past action in progress before another past action: I **had been talking** on the telephone when you interrupted me.

FORMS	
Affirmative	
Had + *been* + progressive form	We **had been planning** our vacation for months.
Negative	
Had + *not* + *been* + progressive form	He **had not been feeling** well.

FUTURE PERFECT PROGRESSIVE

USES
For an action in progress in the future before another future action: She **will have been training** for ten years when she skates in the Olympics.

FORMS	
Affirmative	
Will + *have* + *been* + progressive form	We **will have been driving** for two hours when we reach Kennewick.
Negative	
Will + *not* + *have* + *been* + progressive form	We **will not have been driving** for very long when we reach Boise.
Won't + *have* + *been* + progressive form	We **won't have been driving** for very long when we reach Boise.

2. Irregular Verbs

Base Form	Simple Past	Past Participle
arise	arose	arisen
awake	awoke	awoken
be	was, were	been
bear	bore	borne
beat	beat	beaten/beat
become	became	become
begin	began	begun
bend	bent	bent
bet	bet	bet
bite	bit	bitten
bleed	bled	bled
blow	blew	blown
break	broke	broken
bring	brought	brought
build	built	built
burn	burned/burnt	burned/burnt
burst	burst	burst
buy	bought	bought
catch	caught	caught
choose	chose	chosen
cling	clung	clung
come	came	come
cost	cost	cost
creep	crept	crept
cut	cut	cut
deal	dealt	dealt
dig	dug	dug
dive	dived/dove	dived
do	did	done
draw	drew	drawn
dream	dreamed/dreamt	dreamed/dreamt
drink	drank	drunk
drive	drove	driven
eat	ate	eaten
fall	fell	fallen
feed	fed	fed
feel	felt	felt
fight	fought	fought
find	found	found
fit	fit, fitted	fit, fitted
flee	fled	fled
fling	flung	flung
fly	flew	flown
forbid	forbade/forbad	forbidden/forbade/forbad
forget	forgot	forgotten
forgive	forgave	forgiven

Base Form	Simple Past	Past Participle
forgo	forwent	forgone
freeze	froze	frozen
get	got	gotten/got
give	gave	given
go	went	gone
grind	ground	ground
grow	grew	grown
hang	hung/hanged	hung/hanged
have	had	had
hear	heard	heard
hide	hid	hidden
hit	hit	hit
hold	held	held
hurt	hurt	hurt
keep	kept	kept
kneel	knelt/kneeled	knelt/kneeled
knit	knitted/knit	knitted/knit
know	knew	known
lay	laid	laid
lead	led	led
leap	leapt/leaped	leapt/leaped
leave	left	left
lend	lent	lent
let	let	let
lie (down)	lay	lain
light	lit/lighted	lit/lighted
lose	lost	lost
make	made	made
mean	meant	meant
meet	met	met
pay	paid	paid
prove	proved	proved/proven
put	put	put
quit	quit	quit
read /riʸd/	read /rɛd/	read /rɛd/
ride	rode	ridden
ring	rang	rung
rise	rose	risen
run	ran	run
saw	sawed	sawed/sawn
say	said	said
see	saw	seen
seek	sought	sought
sell	sold	sold
send	sent	sent
set	set	set
sew	sewed	sewn/sewed
shake	shook	shaken
shave	shaved	shaved/shaven
shear	sheared	sheared/shorn
shine	shone/shined	shone/shined

(continued on next page)

Base Form	Simple Past	Past Participle
shoot	shot	shot
show	showed	shown/showed
shrink	shrank/shrunk	shrunk/shrunken
shut	shut	shut
sing	sang	sung
sink	sank	sunk
sit	sat	sat
slay	slew	slain
sleep	slept	slept
slide	slid	slid
sneak	sneaked/snuck	sneaked/snuck
speak	spoke	spoken
speed	sped	sped
spend	spent	spent
spill	spilled/spilt	spilled/spilt
spin	spun	spun
spit	spat/spit	spat/spit
split	split	split
spread	spread	spread
spring	sprang	sprung
stand	stood	stood
steal	stole	stolen
stick	stuck	stuck
sting	stung	stung
stink	stank/stunk	stunk
strew	strewed	strewn
strike	struck	struck/stricken
strive	strove/strived	striven/strived
swear	swore	sworn
sweep	swept	swept
swim	swam	swum
swing	swung	swung
take	took	taken
teach	taught	taught
tear	tore	torn
tell	told	told
think	thought	thought
thrive	thrived/throve	thrived/thriven
throw	threw	thrown
undergo	underwent	undergone
understand	understood	understood
upset	upset	upset
wake	woke/waked	woken/waked
wear	wore	worn
weave	wove	woven
weep	wept	wept
win	won	won
wind	wound	wound
withdraw	withdrew	withdrawn
wring	wrung	wrung
write	wrote	written

3. Common Verbs Usually Used Statively

Appearance
appear
be
concern
indicate
look
mean (= signify)
parallel
represent
resemble
seem
signify (= mean)
sound

Emotions
abhor
admire
adore
appreciate
care
desire
detest
dislike
doubt
empathize
envy
fear
hate
hope
like
love
regret
respect
sympathize
trust

Mental States
agree
amaze
amuse
annoy
assume
astonish
believe
bore
care
consider
deem
deny
disagree
disbelieve
entertain (= amuse)
estimate
expect
fancy
favor
feel (= believe)
figure (= assume)
find
guess
hesitate
hope
imagine
imply
impress
infer
know
mean
mind
presume
realize
recognize
recollect
remember
revere
see (= understand)
suit
suppose
suspect
think (= believe)
tire
understand
wonder

Perception and the Senses
ache
feel
hear
hurt
notice
observe
perceive
see
sense
smart
smell
taste

Possession
belong
contain
have
own
pertain
possess

Wants and Preferences
desire
need
prefer
want
wish

Other
cost
include
lack
matter
owe
refuse
suffice

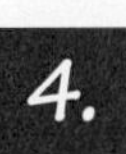

4. Common Uses of Modals and Modal-like Expressions

A. Ability

can	I can speak French.
could	She could talk when she was a year old.
was/were able to	Henry was able to get a scholarship.
will be able to	Sarah will be able to buy a new house.

B. Advice

should	You should study harder.
ought to	You ought to sing in the choir.
should have	You should have acted sooner.
ought to have	We ought not to have said that.
had better	You'd better do something fast.
shall	Shall I continue?[1]

[1]The use of *shall* in a question to ask another's opinion or direction is the only common use of *shall* in American English.

(continued on next page)

C. Certainty: Present and Past

must	He's not here. He must be on his way.
must have	I must have forgotten to pay the bill.

D. Certainty: Future

should	They should be here by nine.
ought to	That ought to help the situation.

E. Expectation: Present and Past

be to	You are to report to the traffic court on April 1.
	He was to be here by nine.
be supposed to	A person accused of a crime is supposed to have a speedy trial.
	The boys were supposed to feed the pets.

F. Futurity

will	He will do it.
shall	I shall never travel again.[2]
be going to	They are going to visit us.
be about to	The bell is about to ring.

G. Habitual Action: Past

used to	I used to procrastinate, but I don't anymore.
would	When I was a child, we would spend every summer at our beach cabin.

H. Habitual Action: Present and Future

will	Many people will gossip if given the chance.

I. Impossibility: Present and Past

can't	This can't be happening.
couldn't	She couldn't be here. I heard she was ill.
can't have	They can't have arrived yet. It's a two-hour trip.
couldn't have	They couldn't have bought a car. They didn't have any money.

J. Lack of Necessity

don't have to	We don't have to leave for work yet.
needn't	You needn't rewrite your essay.

K. Necessity

must	Everyone must pay taxes.
have to	She has to have surgery.
have got to	We've got to do something about the situation.
had to	John had to fly to New York for a meeting.

L. Necessity Not to

mustn't	You mustn't neglect to pay your car insurance.

[2]*Shall* used to express futurity is rare in American English.

M. Opportunity

could	We could go to the park this afternoon.
could have	You could have done better in this course.

N. Possibility

may	He may be sick.
may have	Zelda may have saved enough money.
might	I might go to the play; I'm not sure.
might have	The money might have been stolen.
could	Frank could be on his way.
could have	They could have taken the wrong road.

O. Preference

would rather	Martha would rather stay home tonight than go to the play.

P. Willingness (Volition)

will	I'll help you with your homework.

5. Irregular Noun Plurals

Singular Form	Plural Form
alumna	alumnae
alumnus	alumni
amoeba	amoebas, amoebae
analysis	analyses
antenna	antennas/antennae
appendix	appendices, appendixes
axis	axes
basis	bases
businessman	businessmen
businesswoman	businesswomen
calf	calves
	cattle
child	children
crisis	crises
criterion	criteria
datum	data
deer	deer
dwarf	dwarfs, dwarves
elf	elves
fireman[1]	firemen[1]
fish	fish, fishes[2]
foot	feet
genus	genera

[1]also: firefighter, firefighters

[2]fishes = different species of fish

(continued on next page)

goose	geese
half	halves
index	indexes, indices
knife	knives
leaf	leaves
life	lives
loaf	loaves
louse	lice
mailman[3]	mailmen[3]
man	men
millennium	millenniums, millennia
money	moneys, monies
moose	moose
mouse	mice
octopus	octopuses, octopi
ox	oxen
paramecium	paramecia
	people[4]
phenomenon	phenomena, phenomenons
police officer	police, police officers
policeman	policemen
policewoman	policewomen
postman	postmen[3]
protozoan	protozoa, protozoans
radius	radii, radiuses
series	series
sheaf	sheaves
sheep	sheep
shelf	shelves
species	species
thesis	theses
tooth	teeth
vertebra	vertebrae, vertebras
wharf	wharves, wharfs
wife	wives
woman	women

[3]also: letter carrier, letter carriers

[4]also: person, persons; a people = an ethnic group

6. Some Common Non-Count Nouns

Abstractions

advice
anarchy
behavior
chance
choice
decay
democracy
energy
entertainment
entropy
evil
freedom
fun
good
happiness
hate
hatred
honesty
inertia
integrity
love
luck
momentum
oppression
peace
responsibility
slavery
socialism
spontaneity
stupidity
time
totalitarianism
truth
violence

Activities

badminton
baseball
basketball
billiards
bowling
boxing
canoeing
cards
conversation
cycling
dancing
football
golf
hiking
reading
sailing
singing
soccer
surfing
talk
tennis
volleyball
wrestling

Ailments

AIDS
appendicitis
cancer
chicken pox
cholera
diabetes
flu (influenza)
heart disease
malaria
measles
mumps
polio
smallpox
strep throat

Solid Elements

calcium
carbon
copper
gold
iron
lead
magnesium
platinum
plutonium
radium
silver
tin
titanium
uranium

Gases

air
carbon dioxide
fog
helium
hydrogen
nitrogen
oxygen

Foods

barley
beef
bread
broccoli
cake
candy
chicken
fish
meat
oats
pie
rice
wheat

Liquids

coffee
gasoline
juice
milk
oil
soda
tea
water

Natural Phenomena

aurora australis
aurora borealis
cold
electricity
hail
heat
ice
lightning
mist
rain
sleet
smog
smoke
snow
steam
thunder
warmth

Occupations

banking
computer technology
construction
dentistry
engineering
farming
fishing
law
manufacturing
medicine
nursing
retail
sales
teaching
writing
work

Particles

dust
gravel
pepper
salt
sand
spice
sugar

Subjects

accounting
art
astronomy
biology
business
chemistry
civics
economics
geography
history
Latin
linguistics
literature
mathematics
music
physics
psychology
science
sociology
speech
writing

7. Some Common Ways of Making Non-Count Nouns Countable

Abstractions

a matter of choice
a piece of advice
a piece *or* bit of luck
a type *or* form of entertainment
a unit of energy

Activities

a game of badminton, baseball, basketball, cards, football, golf, soccer, tennis, volleyball
a badminton game, a baseball game, etc.

Foods

a grain of barley
a grain of rice
a loaf of bread
a piece of cake, bread
a piece *or* wedge of pie
a portion *or* serving of—
a slice of bread

Liquids

a can of oil
a can *or* glass of soda
a cup of coffee, tea
a gallon *or* liter of gasoline
a glass of milk, water, juice

Natural Phenomena

a bolt *or* flash of lightning
a clap *or* bolt of thunder
a drop of rain

Particles

a grain of pepper, salt, sand, sugar
a speck of dust

Subjects

a branch of accounting, art, astronomy, biology, business, chemistry, civics, economics, geography, linguistics, literature, mathematics, music, physics, psychology, science, sociology

Miscellaneous

an article of clothing
an article of furniture
an item of news *or* a news item *or* a piece of news
a period of time
a piece of equipment

8. Some Countries Whose Names Contain the Definite Article

The Bahamas
The Cayman Islands*
The Central African Republic
The Channel Islands
The Comoros
The Czech Republic
The Dominican Republic
The Falkland Islands
The Gambia
The Isle of Man
The Leeward Islands
The Maldives
The Marshall Islands
The Netherlands
The Netherlands Antilles
The Philippines
The Solomon Islands
The Turks and Caicos Islands
The United Arab Emirates
The United Kingdom (of Great Britain and Northern Ireland)
The United States (of America)
The Virgin Islands
The Wallis and Futuna Islands

*Some countries are referred to in more than one way—for example, The Cayman Islands *or* The Caymans.

9. Selected Geographical Features and Regions Whose Names Contain the Definite Article

Bodies of Water

The Adriatic Sea
The Aegean Sea
The Antarctic (Ocean)
The Arabian Sea
The Arctic (Ocean)
The Atlantic (Ocean)
The Baltic Sea
The Black Sea
The Caribbean (Sea)
The Caspian Sea
The Gulf of Aden
The Gulf of Mexico
The Gulf of Oman
The Indian (Ocean)
The Ionian Sea
The Mediterranean (Sea)
The North Sea
The Norwegian Sea
The Pacific (Ocean)
The Panama Canal
The Persian Gulf
The Philippine Sea
The Red Sea
The Sea of Japan
The South China Sea
The Strait of Gibraltar
The Strait of Magellan
The Suez Canal
The Yellow Sea

Mountain Ranges

The Alps
The Andes
The Appalachian Mountains
The Atlas Mountains
The Caucasus Mountains
The Himalayas (The Himalayan Mountains)
The Pyrenees
The Rockies
The Urals

Rivers

The Amazon*
The Congo
The Danube
The Ganges
The Hudson
The Mackenzie
The Mississippi
The Niger
The Nile
The Rhine
The Rio Grande
The St. Lawrence
The Seine
The Thames
The Volga
The Yangtze
The Zambezi

*The names of all rivers include the word "river": the Amazon *or* the Amazon River.

Other

The Equator
The Far East
The Middle East (The Near East)
The North Pole
The Occident
The Orient
The Sahara
The South Pole
The Tropic of Cancer
The Tropic of Capricorn

10. Common Verbs Followed by the Gerund (Base Form of Verb + *-ing*)

abhor
acknowledge
admit
advise
allow
appreciate
attempt
avoid
be worth
began
can't bear
can't help
can't stand
celebrate
confess
consider
continue
defend
delay
deny
detest
discontinue
discuss
dislike
dispute
dread
endure
enjoy
escape
evade
explain
fancy
feel like
feign
finish
forgive
give up (= stop)
hate
imagine
justify
keep (= continue)
like
love
mention
mind (= object to)
miss
necessitate
omit
permit
picture
postpone
practice
prefer
prevent
prohibit
propose
quit
recall
recollect
recommend
regret
report
resent
resist
resume
risk
shirk
shun
start
suggest
support
tolerate
understand
urge

11. Common Verbs Followed by the Infinitive (*To* + Base Form of Verb)

afford
agree
appear
arrange
ask
attempt
begin
can't afford
can't bear
can't stand
can't wait
care
chance
choose
claim
come
consent
continue
dare
decide
deserve
determine
elect
endeavor
expect
fail
get
grow (up)
guarantee
hate
hesitate
hope
hurry
incline
intend
learn
like
long
love
manage
mean
need
offer
pay
plan
prefer
prepare
pretend
profess
promise
prove
refuse
request
resolve
say
seek
seem
shudder
start
strive
swear
tend
threaten
turn out
venture
volunteer
want
wish
would like
yearn

12. Verbs Followed by the Gerund or Infinitive with a Considerable Change in Meaning

forget
quit
remember
stop
try

forget
I've almost **forgotten meeting** him. (= At present, I can hardly remember.)
I almost **forgot to meet** him. (= I almost didn't remember to meet him.)

quit
Ella **quit working** at Sloan's. (= She isn't working there any more.)
Ella **quit to work** at Sloan's. (= She quit another job to work at Sloan's.)

remember
Velma **remembered writing** to Bill. (= Velma remembered the activity of writing to Bill.)
Velma **remembered to write** to Bill. (= Velma wrote to Bill. She didn't forget to do it.)

stop
Hank **stopped eating**. (= He stopped the activity of eating.)
Hank **stopped to eat**. (= He stopped doing something else in order to eat.)

try
Martin **tried skiing**. (= Martin sampled the activity of skiing.)
Martin **tried to ski**. (= Martin tried to ski but didn't succeed.)

13. Verbs Followed by Object + Infinitive

advise
allow
ask*
cause
choose*
convince
encourage
expect*
forbid
force
hire
invite
need*
order
pay*
permit
persuade
prepare*
remind
require
teach
tell
urge
want*
warn
would like*

*These verbs can also be followed by the infinitive without an object (example: *want to go* or *want someone to go*).

14. Common Adjectives Followed by the Infinitive

Example:
I was glad to hear about that.

afraid
alarmed
amazed
angry
anxious
ashamed
astonished
careful
curious
delighted
depressed
determined
disappointed
distressed
disturbed
eager
ecstatic
embarrassed
encouraged
excited
fascinated
fortunate
frightened
furious
glad
happy
hesitant
interested
intrigued
lucky
pleased
prepared
proud
ready
relieved
reluctant
sad
scared
shocked
sorry
surprised
touched
upset
willing

15. Common Adjective + Preposition Expressions

Example:
Amanda is fed up with you.

accustomed to
afraid of
amazed at/by
angry at
ashamed of
astonished at/by
aware of
awful at
bad at
bored with/by
capable of
careful of/about
concerned with/about
content with
curious about
different from
excellent at
excited about
famous for
fascinated with/by
fed up with
fond of
furious with
glad about
good at
happy about
interested in
intrigued by/at
mad at (= angry at/with)
nervous about
obsessed with/about
opposed to
pleased about
poor at
ready for
responsible for
sad about
safe from
satisfied with
shocked at/by
sick of
slow at
sorry for/about
surprised at/about/by
terrible at
tired of
used to
weary of
worried about

16. Common Verb + Preposition (or Particle) Combinations

advise against
apologize for
approve of
believe in
choose between/among
come across
complain about
deal with
dream about/of
feel like
figure out
find out
get rid of
insist on
look forward to
object to
plan on
rely on
resort to
run across
run into
stick to
succeed in
talk about
think about
think over
wonder about
write about

17. Spelling Rules for the Progressive and the Gerund

1. Add *-ing* to the base form of the verb.

read	read*ing*
stand	stand*ing*

2. If a verb ends in a silent *-e*, drop the final *-e* and add *-ing*.

leave	leav*ing*
take	tak*ing*

3. In a one-syllable word, if the last three letters are a consonant-vowel-consonant combination (CVC), double the last consonant before adding *-ing*.

CVC
↓↓↓
s i t — sit*ting*

CVC
↓↓↓
r u n — run*ning*

However, do not double the last consonant in words that end in *w, x,* or *y*.

sew	sew*ing*
fix	fix*ing*
enjoy	enjoy*ing*

4. In words of two or more syllables that end in a consonant-vowel-consonant combination, double the last consonant only if the last syllable is stressed.

admít	admit*ting*	(The last syllable is stressed.)
whísper	whisper*ing*	(The last syllable is not stressed, so don't double the *r*.)

5. If a verb ends in *-ie*, change the *ie* to *y* before adding *-ing*.

die	d*ying*

18. Spelling Rules for Nouns and for the Simple Present Tense: Third-Person Singular (*he, she, it*)

1. Add *-s* for most verbs.

work	work*s*
buy	buy*s*
ride	ride*s*
return	return*s*

2. Add *-es* for words that end in *-ch, -s, -sh, -x,* or *-z.*

watch	watch*es*
pass	pass*es*
rush	rush*es*
relax	relax*es*
buzz	buzz*es*

3. Change the *y* to *i* and add *-es* when the base form ends in a consonant + *y.*

study	stud*ies*
hurry	hurr*ies*
dry	dr*ies*

Do not change the *y* when the base form ends in a vowel + *y*. Add *-s.*

play	play*s*
enjoy	enjoy*s*

4. A few verbs have irregular forms.

be	is
do	does
go	goes
have	has

19. Spelling Rules for the Simple Past Tense of Regular Verbs

1. If the verb ends in a consonant, add *-ed*.

return	return*ed*
help	help*ed*

2. If the verb ends in *-e*, add *-d*.

live	live*d*
create	create*d*
die	died

3. In a one-syllable word, if the verb ends in a consonant-vowel-consonant combination (CVC), double the final consonant and add *-ed*.

CVC
↓↓↓
h o p — hop*ped*

CVC
↓↓↓
r u b — rub*bed*

However, do not double one-syllable words ending in *-w*, *-x*, or *-y*.

bow	bow*ed*
mix	mix*ed*
play	play*ed*

4. In words of two or more syllables that end in a consonant-vowel-consonant combination, double the last consonant only if the last syllable is stressed.

prefér	prefer*red*	(The last syllable is stressed.)
vísit	visit*ed*	(The last syllable is not stressed, so don't double the *t*.)

5. If the verb ends in a consonant + *y*, change the *y* to *i* and add *-ed*.

worry	worr*ied*
carry	carr*ied*

6. If the verb ends in a vowel + *y*, add *-ed*. (Do not change the *y* to *i*.)

play	play*ed*
annoy	annoy*ed*

exceptions: pay—paid, lay—laid, say—said

20. Coordinating Conjunctions

and
but
for
nor
or
so
yet

21. Common Subordinating Conjunctions: Single Words and Phrases

after
although
as
as if
as long as
as many as
as much as
as soon as
as though
because
because of the fact that
before
despite the fact that
due to the fact that
even though
however (= the way in which)
if
if only
in case
in spite of the fact that
inasmuch as
no matter if
no matter whether
on account of the fact that
once
plus the fact that
provided (that)
since
so...that
so that
such...that
though
till
unless
until
when
whenever
where
whereas
wherever
whether (or not)
while

22. Transitions: Single Words and Phrases

A. To show an "and" relation

additionally
again
along with this/that
also
alternatively
as a matter of fact
besides (this/that)
by the way
finally
first
for example
for instance
furthermore
in addition
in fact
in other words
in the same way
incidentally
indeed
likewise
that is

B. To show a "but" relation

actually
anyhow
anyway
as a matter of fact
at any rate
despite this/that
even so
however
in any case
in either case
in spite of this/that
instead (of this/that)
nevertheless
nonetheless
on the contrary
on the other hand
rather
still

C. To show a "why/because" relation

accordingly
arising out of this/that
as a result
because of this/that
consequently
for this/that reason
hence
in consequence
in such an event
in this/that case
on account of the fact that
otherwise
then
therefore
this/that being so
thus
to this end

D. To show a time/sequence or other logical relation

after this/that
afterwards
an hour later (several hours later, etc.)
at last
at the same time
at this moment
before this/that
briefly
first(ly)
from now on
henceforth
hitherto
in conclusion
in short
in sum
in summary
in the end
in the meantime
just then
meanwhile
next
on another occasion
previously
second(ly)
then
third(ly), (fourth, fourthly, etc.)
to resume
to return to the point
to summarize
under the circumstances
until then
up to now

23. Verbs and Expressions Followed by the Subjunctive (Base Form)

Examples:
We demand that he do it.
It is essential that he do it.

ask*
demand
insist
it is advisable that
it is crucial that
it is desirable that
it is essential that
it is important that
it is mandatory that
it is necessary that
move (= formally propose in a meeting)
order*
propose
recommend
require*
suggest
urge*

*These verbs also take the form verb + object pronoun + infinitive:
We ask that she be present. *or*
We ask her to be present.

24. Expressions That Can Be Followed by Unreal Conditional Forms

as if
as though
if only
it is time
what if
would rather (that)

Examples:
She acts as if (*or* as though) she were president.
It's time we were leaving.
I'd rather we didn't stay.

25. Pronunciation Table

These are the pronunciation symbols used in this text. Listen to the pronunciation of the key words.

VOWELS

SYMBOL	KEY WORD
iʸ	beat
ɪ	bit
eʸ	bay
ɛ	bet
æ	bat
ɑ	box, car
ɔ	bought, horse
oʷ	bone
ʊ	book
uʷ	boot
ʌ	but
ə	banana, sister
aɪ	by
aʊ	bound
ɔɪ	boy
ɜr	burn
ɪər	beer
ɛər	bare
ʊər	tour

/ṭ/ means that the /t/ sound is said as a voiced sound (like a quick English /d/).

CONSONANTS

SYMBOL	KEY WORD
p	pan
b	ban
t	tip
d	dip
k	cap
g	gap
tʃ	church
dʒ	judge
f	fan
v	van
θ	thing
ð	then
s	sip
z	zip
ʃ	ship
ʒ	measure
h	hot
m	sum
n	sun
ŋ	sung
w	wet
hw	what
l	lot
r	rot
y	yet

From *Longman Dictionary of American English*, © 1983.

Answer Key

Note: In this answer key, where the full form is given, the contracted form is also acceptable. Where the contracted form is given, the full form is also acceptable.

PART V Adverbials and Discourse Connectors

UNIT 12 Adverb Clauses

1.

2. We won't be able to correct the problem of violence unless we treat its underlying causes.
3. Some cartoons contain as much violence as R-rated movies do.
4. Though the drug problem has worsened, there are some positive signs.
5. Some parents curtail their children's TV watching because they think it encourages passivity.
6. There are so few programs of quality on television that some people have gotten rid of their TV sets.
7. Whenever there is an economic downturn, there is a corresponding increase in crime.

2.

because they give students opportunities to be involved in something (why)
on account of the fact that they don't have enough to do to keep themselves busy (why)
so . . . that it's hard to commit a violent act (result)
When their team wins (when)
when their team loses (when)
because they give some students, especially poor ones, an opportunity to get out of a difficult situation and improve their chances for a successful life (why)
If a young basketball player from a poor village in Nigeria can get a scholarship to play for, say, UCLA (under what condition)
than it ever was (comparison)
If a young woman coming from a ghetto is accepted on the University of Missouri swim team (under what condition)
wherever she goes (where)
In spite of the fact that school sporting programs have some deficiencies that need to be ironed out (contrast)
because I'm one of those students (why)

3.

2. Many citizens support gun control because they believe that the easy availability of guns is a key ingredient in violent crime. *or* Because they believe that the easy availability of guns is a key ingredient in violent crime, many citizens support gun control.
3. Many citizens do not support gun control, although they recognize that guns are part of the crime problem. *or* Although they recognize that guns are part of the crime problem, many citizens do not support gun control.
4. Unless teenagers have meaningful activities, they are likely to get involved in crime.
5. There is potential danger wherever we go. *or* Wherever we go, there is potential danger.
6. If criminals commit three serious crimes, they will be sentenced to life in prison without possibility of parole.
7. The Brady Law to control handguns was finally passed after its supporters had lobbied for years for its passage. *or* After its supporters had lobbied for years for its passage, the Brady Law to control handguns was finally passed.
8. While politicians argue about the war on drugs, the drug problem continues to grow. *or* The drug problem continues to grow while politicians argue about the war on drugs.

4.

2. on account of the fact that 3. such . . . that
4. more . . . than 5. as much . . . as
6. In spite of the fact that 7. If

5.

2. The prison escapee was driving so rapidly that he lost control of the car and was apprehended.
3. If they get enough attention from their parents, children probably won't turn to crime.
4. Some children watch so much television *or* such a lot of television that they have trouble telling reality from fantasy.
5. The sheriff's office has put more agents on the streets in case there is additional trouble.
6. Provided their governments appropriate enough money, nations everywhere can gain headway against crime.
7. Today there is more awareness about the underlying causes of violence than there was in the past.
8. Many juvenile criminals today receive light sentences although they commit serious crimes.
9. Today there isn't as much abuse of certain drugs as there used to be. That's a positive sign.
10. In spite of the fact that he had exhibited good behavior, the prisoner was denied parole.

6.

2. a 3. b 4. b 5. a 6. b 7. b 8. a 9. a 10. b

UNIT 13 Adverbials: Viewpoint, Focus, and Negative

1.

Part 1:

2. almost missed
3. Even . . . Nancy
4. only ten
5. Only Eric
6. even lent
7. only wanted
8. only one
9. just wanted
10. just three

Part 2:

2. just 3. simply
4. even, just 5. sadly
6. seldom 7. rarely
8. unfortunately
9. certainly 10. not only
11. only 12. clearly
13. only then

2.

(In some cases, more than three placements are possible.)

2. Unfortunately, violence has increased in public schools. Violence unfortunately has increased in public schools. Violence has increased in public schools, unfortunately.
3. Luckily, some parents are able to spend a great deal of time with their children. Some parents are luckily able to spend a great deal of time with their children. Some parents are able to spend a great deal of time with their children, luckily.
4. Surely, we must be willing to make some sacrifices. We must surely be willing to make some sacrifices. We must be willing to make some sacrifices, surely.
5. Fortunately, some young people manage to survive unhappy childhoods. Some young people fortunately manage to survive unhappy childhoods. Some young people manage to survive unhappy childhoods, fortunately.
6. Evidently, some schools have no policies on bringing guns to campus. Some schools evidently have no policies on bringing guns to campus. Some schools have no policies on bringing guns to campus, evidently.
7. Frankly, it is important to place limits on your children's behavior. It is, frankly, important to place limits on your children's behavior. It is important to place limits on your children's behavior, frankly.

3.

2. I almost got up and called
3. We were only talking
4. guess we just lost
5. simply call and tell
6. Even your little brother
7. called almost
8. just hope you
9. only you can
10. you should even

4.

2. All too seldom do families eat meals together.
3. On no account can domestic violence be ignored.
4. Young people should start paying their own bills. Only then will they begin to truly appreciate their parents.
5. Little does a teenager know about how difficult it is to be a parent.
6. Hardly ever do they understand the need for discipline.

5.

Almost we ➔ We almost
we have ➔ have we
Jonathan got even ➔ even Jonathan got
she takes ➔ does she take
Only we were ➔ We were only
Even they don't ➔ They don't even
I approve ➔ I don't approve
those school officials realize ➔ do those school officials realize
the train comes ➔ comes the train

6.

2. F 3. T 4. T 5. F 6. F 7. F 8. F 9. T

8.

2. b 3. a 4. a 5. b 6. a 7. b 8. a 9. b 10. a

UNIT 14 Other Discourse Connectors

1.

however: contrast so: result Therefore: result
First: relation in time Also: addition so: result
though: contrast In fact: addition then: relation in time
Meanwhile: relation in time so: result however: contrast
for: cause and the sandwich tasted: addition but: contrast
First: relation in time Second: relation in time
Third: relation in time Fourth: relation in time
So: result However: contrast Nonetheless: contrast

2.

2. First 3. second 4. however 5. therefore 6. Also 7. Meanwhile 8. otherwise 9. And 10. In fact

3.

2. However 3. Meanwhile 4. otherwise 5. In fact 6. for example 7. Because of this 8. Nonetheless

4.

in spite of ➔ even though *or* though *or* although *or* in spite of the fact that
however ➔ but
on account of ➔ on account of the fact that
Although ➔ However
besides ➔ and
also ➔ and
Because ➔ Therefore *or* So
Or ➔ Otherwise
also ➔ and
although ➔ however *or* though
otherwise ➔ or

5.

2. b 3. a 4. a 5. b 6. a 7. a 8. b

Adverbial Modifying Phrases

1.

. . .saying that the success of the conference depends on the good faith actions of Mr. Tintor, the country's president.
. . .by agreeing to free and unconditional talks.
Interviewed about Mr. Amalde's comments, . . .
. . .speaking on condition of anonymity, . . .
Acknowledging that the current vaccine is ineffective, . . .
Having conducted successful repairs and identified flaws on Magna Maria, Wasa's existing instrument, . . .
To be known as Illyria, . . .
. . .to be a viable state.

2.

	Subjects	Combine?
2.	standard, problems	no
3.	population, supply	no
4.	Governments, They	yes
5.	parents, people	yes
6.	leaders, citizens	no

3.

2. When giving money to beggars on the street, some tourists mistakenly think they are doing their part to help the poor.
3. Unless provided with firsthand knowledge of poverty, tourists cannot truly understand the plight of the poor.
4. If sponsored by people in wealthier nations, orphans in poor countries can escape the cycle of poverty.
5. Poor people will not be able to escape poverty until given job opportunities.

4.

Incorrect sentences:
By arguing that I don't have enough money anyway, the request is ignored.
Having landed in the capital, a taxi took me to my hotel in the center of town, and that's where I met her.
Sitting on a dirty blanket on the sidewalk in front of the hotel, my eye was caught by her.
While talking later with a nun at a nearby convent that administers gift money from other countries, much worthwhile information was given to me.
Selling her matches, her spirit shone through, simply trying to scratch out a semblance of a living.

5.

2. Given the choice between disaster and some kind of restriction on our right to have as many children as we want, we may have to choose the latter.
3. Having grown slowly between the years 500 and 1700, the world's population then began to accelerate.
4. Clearing more and more land for farms every year, farmers all over the world unfortunately destroy animal habitats.
5. To ensure that their citizens are healthy, many governments provide immunizations to all children.
6. By providing contraceptive devices to their citizens, health officials in some countries are trying to deal with the problem of overpopulation.
7. We must stabilize the world's population growth to prevent ecological disaster.
8. Having witnessed two devastating conflicts in this century, we must do everything in our power to prevent future world wars.

6.

2. Observing that population and food supply grow at different rates, Malthus warned us of a problem.
3. To prevent unrest, governments everywhere must ensure full employment.
4. Having recognized that overpopulation was a problem, the Chinese government took action.
5. Having established a policy of limiting births, Chinese government officials now have to enforce it.
6. Leaders of governments throughout the world must do something comprehensive to prevent a major disaster.
7. If carried out right, the adoption of ZPG would cause the population to decrease.
8. By sponsoring a needy child in the Third World, we make the world a little better.

7.

2. b 3. b 4. b 5. a 6. a 7. a 8. b 9. b 10. b

PART V Review or SelfTest

I.

1. B: as soon as you back the car out of the garage
2. A: than he used to be
   B: unless I threatened him
3. A: when the plane gets in
   B: in case I'm not home
4. A: that I can hardly move
   B: that I end up gaining a few pounds / whenever I come home to visit
5. A: as there used to be
   B: provided that you have cable
6. A: since you didn't turn in your term paper / even though you did well on the tests
   B: because I couldn't think of anything to write about

II.

2. However 3. thus 4. otherwise 5. in fact 6. Moreover

III.

2. Though they had been leaving the children with Sarah's mother, this wasn't a satisfactory situation.
3. One of them was going to have to quit working unless they could find a solution to the problem.
4. When one of their neighbors proposed the creation of a day care co-op involving seven families, their problem was solved.
5. Each day, one of the parents in the co-op cares for all of the children while the other parents are working.

IV.

The even kids ➔ Even the kids
Only I hope ➔ I only hope
almost we didn't ➔ we almost didn't
Little we knew ➔ Little did we know
Never I have been ➔ Never have I been
just we could spend ➔ we could just spend
Never again I will ➔ Never again will I

V.

2. . . . rewards; however, . . .
3. . . . 5:30 P.M., and . . .
4. . . . good, they . . .
5. . . . exercise; also, . . .
6. . . . children, someone . . .
7. . . . until 6:30, and . . .
8. . . . success; none . . .

VI.

2. A 3. C 4. B 5. B 6. C 7. D 8. A

PART V From Grammar to Writing: Sentences and Fragments

A.

F 2. As soon as you learn the hand signals.
S 3. Although China is overpopulated, it is trying to correct the problem.
S 4. We won't solve the problem of violence until we control guns.
F 5. If a young basketball player from Nigeria can get a scholarship.
F 6. Because I was one of those students.
S 7. The economy is perhaps too dependent on the automobile.
S 8. Carried out right, this procedure would cause the population to stabilize.
F 9. By the time the train finally arrived in Santa Maria.
S 10. We need to make some personal sacrifices if we want to help.

B.

company that is
new positions, Dorothy and Patrick
stressful because
on time, they had
a week, they are
work when it is
happier because

C.

2. CX . . . living room, it . . .
3. CPD . . . increase, but natural resources . . .
4. CX no comma
5. S no comma
6. CPD . . . taxes, nor does she . . .
7. CPD . . . at once, for we . . .
8. CX . . . colors, though . . .
9. CX . . . dining car, a violent . . .

D.

Suggested Answers:

2. Although I tried to board the train and find a seat, there wasn't one available.
3. Because heavy rail tracks are already there, heavy rail has gotten the best press.
4. Heavy rail tracks are already there; therefore, heavy rail has gotten the best press.
5. You ran a red light, and you don't seem to know the hand signals.
6. You ran a red light; also, you don't seem to know the hand signals.

PART VI Adjective Clauses

UNIT 16 Review and Expansion

1.

whom others regard as a take-charge leader
who gets things done
who regard the world as their oyster
who is president of her high school class
that benefit everyone
whose behavior is similiar to that of the active-positive in the sense of acting on the world
who is a good example of an active-negative
which is surprising
others regard as a "nice person"
who allows the world to act on him
when he didn't have a lot of friends
one can easily take advantage of
which is what people like about him
where unfortunate things are likely to happen
who is always worried that disaster is just around the corner
that deals with infractions by students

2.

2. which I find somewhat amazing 3. which bothers me
4. which is what everyone likes about him
5. which is mystifying

3.

2. which is why 3. the other prisoners looked up to
4. he's been working for 5. the psychiatrists considered
6. which is why 8. a fact which makes me
9. whom the other prisoners respected
10. for which he has been working
11. whom the psychiatrists considered
12. evidence which makes me

4.

something who we could ➔	something we could *or* something that we could *or* something which we could
tests show ➔	tests that show *or* tests which show
that they tell ➔	that tell
a person whom is ➔	a person who is
things involve ➔	things that involve *or* things which involve
in some way, who doesn't ➔	in some way, which doesn't
guys which live ➔	guys who live

5.

2. b 3. b 4. a 5. b

6.

2. b 3. a 4. b 5. b 6. a

UNIT 17 Adjective Clauses with Quantifiers; Adjectival Modifying Phrases

1.

seen on TV

most of whom answered yes to the question

including the United States, Canada, Mexico, and Japan

regarded as an expert in the field of mass media

most responsible for redirecting our thinking about mediums of communication, especially television

seen on a screen in a movie theater and on a TV set

each of which contains a separate photograph.

projected on the screen

composed of millions of dots

requiring more mental energy

convinced that it leads to mental laziness

many of whom report an almost irresistible tendency to fall asleep while watching television

2.

2. all of whom have played the role of James Bond
3. all of which have earned over $100 million
4. both of which were directed by Akira Kurosawa
5. most of which are loved by children
6. neither of whom is well known to American mass audiences

3.

2. based on Michael Crichton's novel
3. starring John Travolta and Olivia Newton-John
4. directed and produced by Kevin Costner
5. featuring Harrison Ford, Carrie Fisher, and Mark Hamill

4.

2. Westerns, examples of which include *Dances with Wolves*, *Unforgiven*, and *Wyatt Earp,* have been making a comeback in recent years.
3. Musical animated films, including *Aladdin, The Lion King,* and *Beauty and the Beast*, have also become very popular.
4. It looks as though sequels to big movie hits may lose their appeal, in which case moviemakers will be forced to become more creative.

5.

most of them ➔ most of which
illusion is presented ➔ illusion presented
some of them ➔ some of whom
everyone is famous ➔ everyone famous
friends, many of them ➔ friends, many of whom
with a fellow works ➔ with a fellow working
movies are made these days ➔ movies made these days
twists and turns are calculated ➔ twists and turns calculated
in that case ➔ in which case

6.

2. F 3. T 4. F 5. F 6. F 7. T 8. F 9. F 10. T

PART VI Review or SelfTest

I.

I work with in my secretarial job
whom I'll call "Jennifer"
who always greet you in a friendly manner and never have an unkind word to say
whom I'll call "Myrtle"
who rarely gives compliments and can sometimes be critical
who was my friend
which is why I didn't seek out her friendship
when all three of us, Jennifer, Myrtle, and I, were working together
who tends to jump to conclusions
whose name he wouldn't reveal
whom I expected to stand up for me
which was a lie
who had stolen the money
who took the money
that tells us not to judge a book by its cover

II.

2. in which 3. that 4. which 5. most of whom 6. who 7. who 8. whose 9. who 10. whose

III.

2. no change
3. no change
4. (that)
5. no change
6. (that)
7. no change
8. no change

IV.

2. which is why he can be termed an extrovert
3. which is why they often have many friends
4. which is why they tend to value accomplishment
5. which is why they don't always feel satisfied with their accomplishments

V.

2. B 3. C 4. C 5. A 6. D 7. B 8. A 9. D 10. D

PART VI From Grammar to Writing: Punctuation of Adjective Clauses

A.

2. Tom, who is clearly an extrovert, loves meeting new people.
3. Sandra, who is very quick to make friends, loves to have friends over for dinner.
4. Tom and Sandra have two married sons, both of whom live abroad.
5. no change
6. no change
7. no change
8. no change

B.

1. no change
2. no change
3. *The Passenger*, directed by Michelangelo Antonioni and starring Jack Nicholson, is not well known in North America.
4. Many Canadians, including Donald Sutherland and Michael J. Fox, are major international film stars.
5. no change
6. no change

C.

The zoology class, which meets at 8:00 every morning, is . . .
Calculus, which I have at noon every day, looks . . .
There are four of us in our suite, including . . .
Sally, who is from San Antonio, is great; . . .
I also really like Anne, who is . . .
Heather, the other girl from Texas, is . . .

PART VII Noun Clauses and Complementation

UNIT 18 Noun Clauses: Subjects and Objects

1.

it doesn't go nearly far enough
whoever gets something from the nation
what we receive
that it is time to reinvoke John F. Kennedy's famous call to action
what your country can do for you
what you can do for your country
that Congress pass new legislation creating a job corps and requiring all youths to serve in it
whatever they are most skilled at or interested in
Whoever worked in the job corps
What this country needs

2.

2. I'll get a job 3. whatever I'm told 4. whoever hires me
5. I'm going into the army 6. what I want as a career
7. the army will help me decide 8. what I have to do
9. whatever your boss tells you
10. if you might have a point

3.

2. whatever I want 3. whichever one interests me
4. whoever needs help 5. whatever I can
6. however much time you want 7. whoever is
8. whatever needs to be done

4.

Whomever says ➔ Whoever says
That I like ➔ What I like
is what I ➔ is that I
The other thing what ➔ The other thing that
I just wonder that ➔ I just wonder what
I hope what ➔ I hope that

5.

2. a 3. b 4. a 5. b 6. b 7. a 8. a 9. b 10. b 11. a

UNIT 19 Complementation

1.

that the Board of Education isn't taking our concerns seriously
that the board do something positive
that the board sincerely negotiate with us on our request for higher salaries, smaller classes, better discipline, and a real commitment to education
that the board has refused even to talk with us

2.

2. that a lot of the teachers don't want to teach
3. that we are *or* we're there to learn
4. that he or she is there to teach
5. that she would not *or* wouldn't tolerate any nonsense
6. that she was there to help us as much as she could
7. that the whole system needs to be changed

3.

2. It is essential that salaries be raised at least 5 percent per year.
3. It is desirable that teachers be given release time to complete special projects.
4. It is important that no instructor be asked to teach more than five classes per day.
5. It is essential that strict discipline be maintained in the classroom.

4.

players going ➔ players were going
that you were there ➔ that you be there
that you turned in ➔ that you turn in
that we be there ➔ that we were there
that he or she learns ➔ that he or she learn
that fact what ➔ the fact that
People say what ➔ People say that
that teachers like Mrs. Ochoa be ➔ that teachers like Mrs. Ochoa are

5.

2. F 3. T 4. T 5. F 6. F 7. T 8. T 9. F 10. T

PART VII Review or SelfTest

I.

1. B: Whatever you want to do
2. A: where we want to go on vacation
   B: that Hawaii would be nice
3. A: who wins the prize
   B: whoever gets the most points
4. A: she is quilty
   B: the fact that she waited so long to contact the police
5. A: what I'm seeing
   B: that they've been able to do this well
6. A: that I need more time to complete the assignment
   B: Take however long you need to do the job well
7. B: that we need to ban weapons of all kinds
8. B: that she's very unhappy

II.

I report to that's called ➔ I report to what's called
tutor whatever comes in ➔ tutor whoever comes in
I'm amazed what they're ➔ I'm amazed that they're
impressed by who she's learned ➔ impressed by what she's learned
we work on whoever ➔ we work on whatever
that's that we do ➔ that's what we do
for whatever long ➔ for however long

III.

2. where she is
3. that Bill is an asset to our firm, the fact that he's ill a great deal
4. that we need to do, whatever is necessary
5. whoever it is, that it isn't Ron *or* that it's not Ron

IV.

2. C 3. B 4. C 5. A 6. B 7. A 8. D 9. D

PART VII From Grammar to Writing: Writing Direct and Indirect Speech

A.

2. "Sally, how would you evaluate your education?" the reporter queried.
3. "I absolutely despise going to school!" Sally responded.
4. "Jim," Frank said, "you're crazy if you think it's going to be easy to get a job."
5. "Frank," said Jim, "don't be a fool!"
6. The Teachers' Union spokesperson asked the superintendent, "When are you going to start taking our concerns seriously?"

B.

1. Spokesperson Frances Baldwin said that the Board of Education had even refused to talk to them.
2. Board President Bates responded that there was simply no money for salary raises.
3. TV reporter Joan Matthews asked Fumiko if she agreed with Sally that most teachers don't want to teach.
4. Frank asked Jim what he would do if he couldn't find a job after he quit school.
5. Reporter Jim Bresler asked Zeya if she intended to go to college when her term was over.

C.

1. responded
2. commented
3. claimed
4. maintained
5. added

PART VIII Unreal Conditions

UNIT 20 Unreal Conditionals and Other Ways to Express Unreality

1.

if we all paid more attention to our intuitive feelings, we would do better

if a new situation presents itself, you don't have to weigh the evidence on both sides of the question

if you accept the job, you'll soon be bored and will hate it

if you just approach the job with the right attitude, things will turn out well

you end up liking it

as if you liked the work

you hadn't been so hasty

"If only I'd waited a little longer,"

If you'd listened to your intuition, you wouldn't be in this situation

By now you probably would have found a job more to your liking

2.

2. had 3. hadn't been cleaned 4. were *or* was
5. hadn't been changed 6. 'd given up
7. does *or* will do 8. 'd known

3.

2. If the doctor had arrived sooner, he might have been able to save the boy.
3. If the boy had not *or* hadn't been doing a man's job, he probably wouldn't have been killed.
4. If the saw had cut the boy's finger instead of his hand, the boy could probably have survived.
5. The boy might not have been cut by the saw if the sister hadn't said "supper" at a crucial moment.
6. If the work boss had said "Call it a day," the boy would have escaped his fate.
8. The doctor probably wishes (that) he had *or* he'd arrived sooner.
9. The boy's parents probably wish (that) they had not *or* hadn't allowed the boy to work at a man's job.
10. Other parents probably hope (that) this kind of accident does not (doesn't) *or* will not (won't) happen to their children.

4.

world owe her → world owed her
wish she won't → wish she wouldn't
If I would have → If I had
I might had → I might have
probably would get → probably would have gotten
if I would have → if I had
If only I wouldn't have → If only I hadn't
hope she never asked → hope she never asks
hope I didn't agree → hope I don't agree

5.

2. b 3. b 4. a 5. b 6. a 7. a 8. b 9. a 10. a

UNIT 21 Inverted and Implied Conditionals; Subjunctive in Noun Clauses

1.

Subjunctive verb forms:
(that she) come, get
(that Mary) look into

Implied conditionals:
If so . . .
With a little bit of practice . . .

2.

2. let 3. got 4. started 5. were

3.

2. her way be considered 3. an argument be won
4. an argument be fair 5. you adopt
6. you give 7. something be done
8. a course of action be followed

4.

2. had she stayed 3. otherwise 4. with 5. If so 6. If not
8. if she had stayed 9. if she didn't find work 10. if she had
11. if they were hiring 12. if they weren't hiring

5.

essential that I found ➔ essential that I find
(essential that I) just came ➔ (essential that I) just come
Had I know ➔ Had I known
as if I have ➔ as if I had
as if I be ➔ as if I were *or* am
it's time I'm telling ➔ it's time I told
What if I had come ➔ What if I came

6.

Comprehension
2. F 3. F 4. T 5. F 6. T 7. T 8. F 9. T 10. F 11. F

Optional Dictation
2. that you keep 3. demands that he take 4. that he have
5. as if she owned 6. were 7. 'd rather she didn't
8. important that we not excite 9. It's time you took
10. I were you I'd sit down 11. 'd insist that he find
12. What if he were to 13. suggest that you give

PART VIII Review or SelfTest

I.

2. If he had changed the oil, the engine wouldn't have seized.
3. If the engine hadn't seized, the other car wouldn't have rear-ended him.
4. He wouldn't have had to pay a towing bill.
5. He wouldn't have had to replace the engine.
6. He could have made it to the job interview if all this hadn't happened.
7. If he had made it to the job interview, he might have gotten the job.
8. Brandon hopes that he has learned his lesson.

II.

2. as though it were going to 3. as if he were
4. as though he had been 5. as if she were
6. as though you thought

III.

2. not lose her temper 3. bring the dog in at night
4. get rid of the animal
5. call the animal control bureau

IV.

2. we'd realized 3. he keeps *or* he'll keep
4. there's *or* there will be 5. we could contact
6. weren't 7. we had
8. this won't be *or* this isn't
9. we knew 10. it is *or* it will be

V.

2. B 3. A 4. C 5. A 6. C 7. A 8. D 9. B 10. D

PART VIII From Grammar to Writing: Avoiding Run-on Sentences and Comma Splices

A.

2. Thain asked Aurora to pull over; his intuition told him the old man needed their help.
3. Kate knew she had to change her relationship with her boss, but she didn't know how to do it.
4. Although *or* Though *or* Even though Aurora wished they had gotten to the yard sale on time, she was glad they had stopped to help the old man.

B.

2. Thain and Aurora drove to a pharmacy. They got the old man his insulin.
3. Aurora wanted to get to the yard sale; there was a chest of drawers for sale.
4. Aurora didn't want to stop for the old man, but Thain persuaded her it was necessary.
5. Although *or* Though *or* Even though Harold says he will seek professional help to overcome his anger, there is no assurance that he will carry out his promise.
6. Feeling dominated by her mother-in-law, Nancy needed to take assertive action.

C.

2. Nancy says she wants to do something worthwhile. If so, she should join the Peace Corps.
3. I need to get a bank loan; otherwise, I'll have to file for bankruptcy.
4. Jack and Margo would like to send James to a private school. However, the school is expensive, and James doesn't want to go.
5. Becky and David love their new neighborhood; in fact, they're going to buy a house there.

D.

Note: The periods and semicolons below can be interchanged so long as the capitalization is correct.

. . . it works. Last summer . . .
. . . I work. We interviewed . . .
. . . Sarah. On paper, Bob . . .
. . . better qualified; he had . . .
. . . job. However, Sarah . . .
. . . impressed us. She . . .
. . . simply. Bob . . .
. . . everything. All of us . . .
. . . Sarah better. In fact . . .
. . . wasn't wrong; she's turned . . .

Index